HUMOUR●LOGY

The Serious Business of Humour at Work

I love Ludlow!

Paul Boross

Live. Love. Laugh.

Best wishes.

GeniusMedia
CREATING KNOWLEDGE

2023

Humourology

The Serious Business of Humour at Work

First Edition: June 2023 v1.6

ISBN 978-1-90829363-3

Genius Media

B1502

PO Box 15113

Birmingham

B2 2NJ

www.geniusmedia.pub

books@geniusmedia.pub

www.paulboross.com

Humourology

1 A Man Walks Into a Bar...4

2 Step Into My Office...18

    Leadership...22

    Culture...31

    Sales..41

    Presenting...47

    Networking..56

    Interviewing...61

    Negotiating..64

    Coaching..67

    Learning...73

    Team building..76

    Organisational change....................................82

    Creativity..87

    Wellbeing...93

3 Bouncing Back..102

    How to keep your chin up...............................111

    Failure is definitely an option..........................117

    All the world's a stage....................................128

    Kindness..131

4 Growing Your Funny Bone....................................136

    Finding the line...156

    Sitting it out...157

    A funny thing happened.................................162

    A problem shared. 165

    State the obvious..167

5 The Punchline...172

    Acknowledgements.......................................177

    The Humourology Podcast...............................179

    About Paul...183

6 References..188

A Man Walks Into a Bar

"Humour is a social lubricant."

John Sweeney

You have a great sense of humour. In fact, you are funnier than many of the people you know. Your sense of humour is sophisticated and you have the ability to see the funny side of situations that cause others to throw in the towel. You may or may not consider yourself a joke-teller or a clown, yet you have a sense of humour which has carried you through many sticky situations in life.

The average person spends over 3,500 days at work during their lifetime[1]. Presumably, at some point, a sense of humour must come in handy on at least a few of those days. More than that, a well developed sense of humour is your most valuable defence against the trials and troubles of the world. Your ability to weather any storm, to bounce back from setbacks, to get knocked down seven times and get up eight is thanks to your innate ability to see failure as an opportunity, to look back on the hard times and reflect on what you've learned, to smooth the rough edges and soften the bumps in the road. Good humour creates resilience[2].

Humourology is the art and science of using humour to create a competitive advantage. A sense of humour is your most important asset in surviving an increasingly complex and challenging world. A sense of humour increases your mental resilience and makes your more likeable and these two things together will make your success in life, and in business, inevitable. Humourology will take your natural sense of humour and amplify it so that you can use at the right times in your life and work.

I'm sure you've also seen someone attempt to use humour at the wrong time, in the wrong situation. I'm sure you've cringed at a feeble icebreaker during a presentation. Maybe you've even felt a little awkward yourself at times.

We're born with a sense of humour as one of our innate social skills. Yes, we're born with these skills, and at the same time, there's no doubt that some people have devoted their lives to developing those skills, refining them to an art form. We happily pay money to be entertained, in comedy clubs, at the cinema, at the theatre, even through music that makes us laugh. As TV presenter Dermot Murnaghan puts it, "Humour is essential, it lubricates human relations."

We pay to laugh because laughter is valuable. It bonds us, connects us, brings us together. Laughter builds trust. If we laugh at the same jokes, we must share the same life experiences. 'In' jokes identify outsiders.

Life President of Comic Relief and founder of Sport Relief Kevin Cahill knows very well the power of humour to bring people together. "All communities have the ability to laugh but what's interesting is certain types of humour, such as slapstick, generally work in most cultural contexts and for most communities."

Whilst we're born with a sense of humour, your own style and preference is of course influenced by your unique upbringing. Comedian, presenter and writer Arthur Smith recalls just such an influence. "I learned early on that humour was my thing and could make me popular. At primary school, we performed *Peter Pan*. Obviously I was Captain Hook. I came out shouting and being scary, or I so thought, but everybody started laughing. The scarier I tried to be, the more they laughed. I realised that people laughing at me was good. I liked it."

TV presenter and chef Ainsley Harriott is known for his loud, energetic, gregarious style which he attributes to his parents who combined a social life built around food with the energy and joy of the entertainment world. "We are a product of our parents, they bring us into the world. My mother was an absolute, superb cook and a wonderful entertainer and in her own way as far as her family were concerned, there was laughter, there was energy in the house and there was this lovely banter. That's what you grew up with. You grew up with that energy and it revolved around food. I used to sit in the front room, underneath the table and just look up at all of his friends and people that were coming round, some of them famous names, like Bob Monkhouse, they were all in show business together. No one was above their station, they all did gigs, that was their career and they'd all come and I'd hang around with them. Some of them that hadn't made it big on TV, and my mum would come in with bits of food on the tray and I'd have a bit of a drink. She'd make a little punch or around Christmas time eggnog or something like that. Just lovely stuff, and all of that combined together is part of my makeup. The laughter, the joy, the cooking and everything, and the exuberance, their personalities, your personality. If you're growing up with that banter, it comes easier. You can fit in easier because if you can tease you can play. Playing is one of those things that you do best when you play with people, you will tease, you will banter with them, you'll cajole them."

Not everyone was born into a family of entertainers and you certainly don't need that upbringing in order to have a sense of humour. Yours will have developed naturally from whatever experiences you were exposed to in life and it will have been further refined as you found your way through the world of work. Comedian, writer and former TV executive Cally Beaton says, "I wouldn't say there was a lot of laughter in my household. My family are quite intellectual and bookish, and I wasn't quite so much like that. I did go to an all boys school because that was the school my parents taught at and we lived in the grounds of that school. It was a private school and so I was educated there. If you are the only girl in an all boys school at the age of eight, and you happen to be overweight with ginger hair then you do need to develop quite the personality to combat a feeling of not belonging. I developed a sense of humour, or certainly a capacity to exude humour as a child."

Actor, comedian and writer Omid Djalili similarly developed his comedy skills in order to survive as a cultural outsider. "I learned that humour is like a superpower. I remember doing a sketch at school in front of the whole school. There were these very cool girls who were saying 'you're funny, hang around with us'. So they would look for me at break time and I got to sit with them. I realised that this goofy, ugly Iranian kid can win over a whole school with a fabulous punch line. I learned that humour was one way to sublimate being an ethnic minority being not just ignored, but maybe pilloried because the Iranian revolution happened and they were showing lots of images of Islamic fundamentalists and we look like a very, very unattractive bunch of people to hang around with. Yet, it was an Iranian kid that made the whole school laugh. It was a big moment in my life."

Dame Arlene Phillips CBE is a choreographer, presenter, theatre director and former dancer, known for her role as a judge on the TV show *Strictly Come Dancing*.

"I never thought of humour at all in my family but I do remember my father laughing. Anything he saw of Charlie Chaplin, he would be on the floor laughing, yet one would think that my father was actually quite a serious man, he'd had a tough life. Thrown out of home at twelve years old, by the archetypal wicked stepmother who had her own son. My father's mother died when he was very young, two years old and so the step mother came in and she had her own child and that was time for my father to go, so he carried the weight of the world. It took a Buster Keaton or Charlie Chaplin to make him laugh. There wasn't a lot of humour in the air so to me, laughter was something you had to see, to experience."

Film-maker, comedian, writer, actor and TV presenter Danny Wallace's upbringing was different again, yet with no less emphasis on humour. "I was always drawn to humour and I listened to comedy, rather than music. A lot of the time, I'd go to bed listening to *Fawlty Towers*, or Tom Lehrer on an auto reverse cassette or *Blackadder*, the audio versions. When I heard Tom Lehrer, I had very little idea what he was talking about half the time, because it would be about Verner von Braun and the politics of missiles in the late 1960s. I didn't know what it was about but I listened to his timing, I listened to the audience and I listened to the individual laughs and the mastery, the control he had over them and the talent he had."

In the nature versus nurture debate, the nurture can come from anywhere. It doesn't have to be a family of stage performers, it could be from friends, teachers, even just favourite TV and radio shows. You have a sense of humour and some set of events shaped that to create your unique personality.

Danny continues with some thoughts about his mother and his early life. "My mum is an incredibly golden hearted and social woman who sees the best in everybody. There was an old man where we lived called Mr. Montgomery. He would get so angry at me and my friends when we were playing football. He always had all these plants outside his porch, loads of them. I created a letterhead for the 'Hay Fever Sufferers of the UK United Alliance' and wrote a letter to Mr. Montgomery, saying that one of our representatives had been in the local area, and had done a pollen count outside his porch and found it to exceed the national average by some degree and that he was from now on to limit the number of pot plants in his porch to either six large or eight small or further action would be taken. I put it through his door and pretended it was from my friend Simon, who was head of the UK hay fever people. He phoned Simon in a rage but sadly, he got through to Simon's mum, who didn't understand what was going on, and assumed that Simon had been kidnapped and this mad old man was part of some kind of plot. When she phoned me to ask me if I was responsible, my stomach dropped and I knew I'd done the worst thing that any human being had ever done, ever. This was an atrocity of unknown and epic proportions. I thought, I've got to tell mum so I said, 'Mum, I've done something really bad. You know, Mr. Montgomery...' and then I tell her about the letter, and I tell her about the plants and I tell her how angry he was. I wanted to look up, I couldn't, I thought she was hurt. She was crying with laughter. She said it was brilliant. I thought I was going to get into trouble with everybody but instead, my mum just encouraged that kind of stuff and my dad thought it was great as well because he didn't like Mr. Montgomery, who was often leaving notes on our car. So I was encouraged to do elaborate things by these people, nature and nurture both played their part."

What an incredibly diverse range of experiences create our sense of humour. You don't have to be born into a family of professional comedians to be funny, it seems to be something which naturally emerges in any upbringing, often as a way of coping with life's troubles.

I know what you're thinking. How is this going to help me in business? Tell a few jokes in a sales meeting? Laugh in the face of failure? See off your enemies with a witty one-liner, James Bond style?

Yes, that's pretty much it and in this book, I'm going to show you two extremely important things. Firstly, exactly how humour will pay off in your business and career. Secondly, how to develop your sense of humour so that you become a finely honed weapon of mass amusement. Or at least, able to hold your own at dinner parties, board meetings, networking events and other assorted soirées.

In business, it's no longer survival of the fittest, it's survival of the funniest.

Tessy Ojo CBE is the Chief Executive of the Diana Award, a NED of Comic Relief, BBC Charity Appeals and more as well as a forceful campaigner for social justice. "I want my team to thrive, I want my team to feel that they have all the tools they need to come into the workplace. If we could successfully support the team through intentional laughter, I know three things will happen, I will increase my team's mental well being, I will improve their general levels of happiness, and which invariably improves their levels of engagement. But also, I would reduce sick days. If they're happier, healthier, they would take less time off.

The finance director wants productive days, obviously, but what is the point of a business without its staff? You need to have a vision where you have unique people, where your people matter. One of the things that really struck me the most in the pandemic was how much people matter. A business without its people is nothing. Our people need to be well, they need to be engaged. We want to be an employer of choice. We want people to choose us. We want to have an employer value proposition that includes 'we will look after your mental well being' and so those things are so important to us as an organisation that anything that supports our staff members to thrive mentally and physically is a priority for us."

OK, so if we make people laugh at work, they'll work harder and we'll make more money?

Well, yes, I suppose that is the case, but it's much more than that too. In any case, money isn't a bad thing because it enables a business to pay people so that they can take care of their families and do the things that they love doing.

We both know that it's just not feasible to have people laughing all day because they would never get any work done. Thus, the science of Humourology is in leveraging the structure of humour to enable human interactions to function more effectively, whilst the art of Humourology is in achieving that whilst actually still being funny.

Every good joke has two main parts to it; the setup and the punchline. The setup creates the context, sets the scene. "A man walks into a bar" tells you everything that you need to know - if you have ever seen a man, or a bar, that is. Even the setup creates a connection between us.

The punchline creates conflict, and the conflict between the expected and the unexpected, the familiar and the unfamiliar, the known and the unknown creates emotional tension, and you release that tension by laughing, or at the very least, smiling politely.

A man walks into a bar… and says, "Ouch!"

OK, I admit, that might not seem funny now, in the cold light of day, but I guarantee you'll have told that joke to your friends and colleagues by the time you've reached the end of this book. Why? Because you seek social acceptance, you crave connection. You want to be liked, to enjoy the safety of the social group, and I just gave you a watertight, guaranteed, proven way to achieve that.

According to research from Professor Richard Wiseman[3], we love the terrible jokes in Christmas crackers precisely because they are terrible. If the joke is too funny, it becomes selective. Some people will get it, and the ones who don't will feel alienated. By making the joke awful, everyone gets it, and everyone feels included. It might be the kind of joke that you groan at rather than laugh at, but the point is that you all groan together, and then you laugh about the fact that you all groaned together. If you have ever been in a room full of people groaning together then you should probably keep that to yourself, or at least invite me next time.

OK, so we know what it means to be funny, and we're starting to understand the immense social value of humour. What about the business value?

Business owners are under continual pressure to streamline, to cut costs, to increase efficiency, to mass produce, to go online, to automate, to replace expensive people with cheap robots. The automation of the workplace pushes human beings into more specialised roles where robots and AIs simply cannot compete. Roles involving creativity, complex decision making, emotional connection and the uniqueness of human interaction become more and more valuable as less 'human' tasks become increasingly automated.

In commodity sales, the trend is towards automation and self service. However, the higher the sales value, the more we need human beings to build relationships, understand the customer's needs and differentiate products and services.

I'm sure that if you're trying to make a change to your home insurance policy, you don't want to wait in a call centre queue for 45 minutes to speak to an operator. However, when you're buying a new car, you want to feel understood and valued, you want the full coffee and chocolate biscuit experience. 45 minutes treated like a VIP is time well spent.

There isn't a single area of business that I can think of where the working relationship isn't improved with good humour.

I often see social media posts about how consumer facing companies have demonstrated good customer service with humour, ranging from amusing complaint responses to witty digs at competitors, and of course there are many well known advertising campaigns which aim to be memorable by being funny. There are even late night TV shows dedicated to reminiscing over the best, featuring 'talking heads' comedians to tell us why they're funny.

The act of smiling releases hormones which fight stress. Dopamine, endorphins and serotonin are all released which not only relaxes your body, it can also lower your heart rate and blood pressure. Endorphins also act as a natural pain reliever and the serotonin release brought on by your smile serves as an anti-depressant and mood lifter.

Dame Arlene Phillips knows about the beneficial effects of endorphins too. "I am totally keen on trying to give everyone the opportunity to express themselves, everyone to have an opportunity to feel that they can they can get involved. Lightness and humour in a workplace are definitely beneficial. Humour and laughter are good for the endorphins. Without question, you release things so much, by just allowing yourself to laugh and everybody else to laugh."

Smiling is a social signal too, so a smile not only makes you feel good, it makes the people around you feel good too. Researchers at the Face Research Laboratory at the University of Aberdeen, Scotland asked subjects to rate smiling and attractiveness. They found that both men and women were more attracted to images of people who made eye contact and smiled than those who did not. As much as you would like to believe that it's the fabulous features and benefits of your product that your customers are buying into, it's also your winning smile that has them reaching for the 'buy now' button.

Humour is memorable, and in business, it's rarely the 'best' product or service which wins, it's rarely the 'best' candidate who gets the top job. Why not? Because 'best' is almost impossible to quantify. There are so many variables that can't be controlled. But at the end of the day, every decision in business is a human decision. Just take a moment to remember some of the times that you turned down what seemed like the objectively 'best' option and went with your gut, or your heart. Did you buy the car that had the better economy and the lower insurance, or the one you loved the feel of? Did you choose the job that paid better or the one you felt a connection with? Did you buy the house that was more for your money, or the one which felt like home?

Every decision is a human decision. Humans are very, very bad at analysing objectively. We are inherently subjective. I find it interesting that recruiters and corporate buyers try to take the emotion out of their decisions whilst advertisers and artists try to create as much of an emotional connection as possible.

We are unable to choose the best option, and whilst sometimes that's because manufacturers and retailers make it impossible for us to compare apples with apples, it's also because every decision that we make is a compromise, and in the end, we choose with our hearts, not our minds.

Being able to make a connection with another person is the essence of success in any walk of life. It's easy to think that your success is because of your knowledge, your skills, your business instincts, but you can't achieve much by yourself - something which Cally Beaton learned in her time as a TV executive. "Everything you do professionally is about human connection. When I was bringing in multi millions of dollars of revenue at Viacom, I didn't believe that I was a brilliant negotiator or a brilliant business person, I just knew how to connect with people, and they wanted to work with me and or for me or with me, and that's the only thing I've ever been any good at. That's what comedians need to do, right? We've got to get onto a stage and connect."

Every decision is a human decision. Did I mention that yet? We can't choose what's best, so we choose what feels safest, and safest means most familiar, and most familiar means most memorable, and human beings remember best when they feel an emotional connection.

You could make your customers feel disgusted or angry or scared. That would certainly be memorable. But if you can make them laugh, you're memorable for all the right reasons.

After all, wouldn't you rather be able to go home at the end of every working day and say, "I had fun today"?

Laughter is a social currency. It's a bond. It's a gift meant to be shared. Laughing together means that we share values, we share life experiences, we share hopes and dreams. Laughing together creates a connection that can last a lifetime.

Humourology is simply the art and science which enables you to take that special, human connection and turn it into a competitive advantage.

2 Step Into My Office

"If it isn't fun, why would you do it?"

David McCourt

In this section of the book, I'm going to explore a number of areas of business life and show you both how and why humour is such a powerful asset and an important ingredient in your recipe for success.

I'm sure that you can think of other areas of business where humour is valuable, so what I've aimed to do here is to look at areas where the quality of human relationships is the most important differentiator and creator of value. Of course, you need other things too; good products or services, sound financial management, innovation, market intelligence, well-organised sales processes and so on. Yet without human relationships, none of these would make any difference.

Actor Michael Fenton Stevens says, "The jobs I enjoyed the most are the ones I had the most fun in, not just because I was messing about, often the work can be very hard and very serious. The idea that somebody making a joke is a waste of time because 'We've got to get on with this' is not true. When things are getting too serious, humour can get you out of all those situations."

Humour crops up in any business interaction involving people, so rather than explore this in general, I have attempted to condense the infinite variety of workplace whimsy and job japes into a number of categories which I hope cover the majority of working situations that you might find yourself in need of a lighter perspective.

What I would say before I begin is that it's worth remembering that all humour has some foundation in honesty. The court jester is a figure who could poke fun at the establishment in order to deliver honesty in a way which would be rejected if anyone else did it. The word that we use to describe such entertainment today is 'satire', and at least in relation to the world of work, one of the best known examples of work based satire in recent years is the TV show The Office.

TV producer and one time BBC Head of Comedy Jon Plowman had the honour of meeting the creators of the show when they were pitching the idea. "Two people walk into my office. One was a tall, thin guy, and one was short and fat. The tall thin guy had been doing the BBC directors course and the short fat guy had been in a band but hadn't really made an impact. They had an idea that they had touted around to everybody. They showed me the beginning of of the idea, they made a short piece in which the short fat guy was trying to get somebody into his company without doing the required safety exams to do with forklift trucks. At one point, he says, 'fork lift truck exams, I write them' and he does a Pinocchio nose. Those two people were Ricky Gervais and Stephen Merchant, the show they were offering me to which I unbelievably said yes was *The Office*. What I said was, 'look, it's fine, but I don't understand why this company employ this guy, David Brent, who's incompetent, not very good at his job. Why do they employ him?' He said, 'Jon, can I take you for a walk around the BBC?' The implication was that he was going to show me, in every department of the BBC, people similar to David Brent, and he may have been right.

We took it to the controller of BBC2 and she worried about it a bit because at the time, there were quite a number of shows on BBC2, that were 'Docusoaps', they were things like 'Hotel', 'Shop', 'Airport', they were documentaries spun out to a number of weeks, in which they tried to make characters out of the ordinary people working in ordinary jobs. She was slightly worried that if the office caught on, it would kill off those shows. It did quite well on its on its first week. Not great, but quite well. It dipped, which is what all comedies do, then in its last couple of weeks, it picked up a little bit. *The Office* didn't do that. It just went along the bottom and then picked up enough for her to think, 'Hang on, maybe this is word of mouth. This is people watching it, realising what it is because a show called *The Office* might sound boring. There's no reason why *The Office* should be funnier than The Hotel. She had the courage to repeat it and the repeat doubled its audience. Most shows don't do that. So it was a sign of faith on her part and faith that the audience came to love it."

Perhaps nobody wanted to watch another reality TV show about life in an office when they were already living in a reality show called 'work', yet as soon as they realise that they show was a satire, a parody, its value soared.

You don't have to create a hit TV show to turn humour into a competitive advantage, so let's put the fun back into business fundamentals and add a punchline to the bottom line.

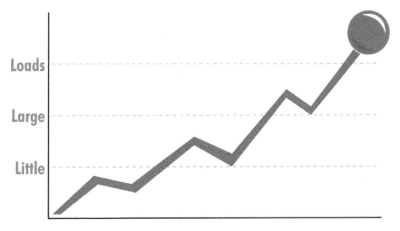

Leadership

Research shows that leaders with even a meagre sense of humour are viewed as 27% more motivating and admired[4] than those who don't use humour. Their teams are 15% more engaged and are more than twice as likely to solve a creativity challenge.

Georgie Holt is the UK managing director of Acast, a global podcast publishing and distribution platform. She says, "Good leaders and good businesses should want happy, healthy, relaxed staff. Because that is where not only do you get the best out of people, the best teams are formed, the best results are created for whatever industry you're in. In a socially distanced workplace, you have to invest in things that are going to bring you together. For most people, laughter is a great way to do that. If you can find the humour, it can build resilience in teams and in yourself. Because if you're trying to seek out the funny, then your chances are you're going to bounce back. It's about healthy, happy staff who are emotionally available for one another in the good times and the bad. Retention is about people who want to stay with you for the course and for the journey in the good times and in the tougher times. Staff well-being and teams that are confident and want to create positive change and do good work and do good things. Laughter is something that connects all of those ambitions, and certainly something that can move tough situations on quite quickly. Evolution has been about survival. It's about creating social bonds that help us to survive and feel part of a community, a tribe, a social group, which enables survival over time. Laughter is essential for human survival."

We could perhaps trace the origins of humour in leadership to the role of the court jester, a history which spans many thousands of years and certainly dates back to the courts of the Egyptian Pharaohs and Roman Emperors.

Historian and TV presenter Dan Snow notes that satirical theatre was another important way in which people broke down the barriers between classes. "Look at ancient Athens, the plays written and performed. Satire and humour were the staple, they cut the big citizens down to size. The political satire was a way for the little people to get back at their overmighty overlords.

Throughout history, humour has been essential, and it's often quoted that the minute you start laughing at someone, you stop fearing them. Laughter is a very, very potent weapon."

We might say that the role of the jester was not only to entertain the court but also to offer a relief to the tension which inevitably builds up around a government which can't please all of the people, all of the time. In this modern day and age, it would at least be nice to have a government which pleased some of the people, some of the time, but that's probably why I don't perform political satire any more.

The jester would poke fun at the monarch in order to share, in an indirect way, feedback from 'ordinary people'. The jester's role often became that of an unofficial advisor, able, through the veil of humour, to say things that other courtiers and officials would be afraid to say.

Through humour, the jester offered a valuable reality check.

Today, this important, supportively critical role is played by the 'office joker' who might mimic the boss or perhaps draw caricatures, or even by corporate entertainers who are hired to speak at annual conferences. Comedian and impressionist Alistair McGowan says, "I've been surprised sometimes doing corporate events where the head of the organisation will introduce me after they've made quite a lengthy speech, and that's always great fun because, if they've got a doable voice, you've only got to give a representation of it, a replication of it and people love it because you're doing the boss. Obviously you're respectful to him, but he doesn't have the status that he does for the staff."

I heard that Jonathan Ross was hired for a corporate event by the Rank Organisation, and if you don't know Jonathan, one of his trademarks is his tendency to pronounce 'r' as 'w', thereby creating much amusement for the audience as the leaders of the organisation used Jonathan in the role of the court jester, to humanise the monarchy, to ease any conflict, open up lines of communication and simply give everyone a jolly good laugh. The leader who can laugh at themselves has huge power, and if they can also allow others to laugh along too, that power is amplified.

The system of British politics relies on adversarial debate, and successful politicians incorporate humour as a powerful way to bring the discussion back to Earth. British politician William Hague is particularly fond of this approach. "It works a lot in democracies, particularly those with a good tradition of humour in public life, and we are certainly one of those. My favourite period of history is the 18th century, I've written books about William Pitt, the younger, who was Prime Minister then. There was so much humour and irreverence directed, in those days, at political leaders, even at the Royal Family, much ruder, much more vulgar cartoons and press commentary than we experience today, that we would think were unacceptable today in the mainstream press. It's one of the reasons we have a healthy democracy, because we couldn't take a dictator seriously. We would have made pitiless fun of them before they got to the position of having too much power. Political humour always has to be within within the parameters of what society finds humorous at the time, but there's lots of scope in any age to puncture the pomposity of an over mighty leader."

Of course, it's also important not to go too far, as comedian Neil Mullarkey agrees. "I don't think you want David Brent running every team. Now, he wasn't self aware enough, but just allowing laughter, the dry humour, the quiet humour. When somebody says something, the boss laughing is great because everyone looks, is that okay? Was that wrong? The generosity of the audience is as much a thing as the maker of the joke."

Broadcaster and author René Carayol adds, "A tough, fast-paced stressful, highly competitive, difficult, ambiguous world which is quite unforgiving, that's a tough place to walk into every day. Knowing that you're going to be amongst a bunch of people who don't take themselves too seriously, who will take time out to just laugh at themselves laugh with each other, and just care for each other? How fabulous. At the moment, as many of us are working from home, it's even more important. Checking in to see how someone is and having a moment to just see you, have a laugh, bit of brevity, break some of the monotony of the moment, especially if it's from your line manager. How wonderful is that? They're not coming in to say how's the KPIs, how's the old profit line but to just have a laugh and laugh at themselves? If the boss laughs at themselves, everyone relaxes a little bit more, tries a little bit harder."

William Hague shares an example of someone who didn't routinely make use of humour - Margaret Thatcher. "Not everybody is funny in their daily dealings. Margaret Thatcher was not funny. That was not her approach. She was, in my view, an extremely impressive, brilliant person in so many ways and everybody, whatever their political views, would say she was a major figure in history and an important leader. But she wasn't funny, she didn't react well to humour, because she didn't really get it. She would enjoy having an argument, she would enjoy having a discussion. But whereas many people would inject some humour into it, help it along, that just wasn't her approach at all. You can be successful without humour but it does create a pretty serious atmosphere around you and you had better have some other massive attributes, if you're going to do without it."

So it's possible to be successful without humour, but it takes much, much more effort.

William Hague goes on to share a contrasting story about Hillary Clinton. "We'd been sitting at the same table for a NATO meeting for about eight hours. When you have a meeting of the foreign ministers of all the NATO member states, they all want to say something. Imagine if you have four or five different topics and 29 people want to say something and they're all very serious subjects in a military alliance. Well, you've been there about eight hours, and you're all jet lagged and in a strange country.

Of course you feel like it is a human thing to think we need to relax a bit. We need to look at the world in a slightly different way. The United Kingdom always sits next to the United States. for alphabetical reasons at such meetings. I remember Hillary leaning across to me and she said, 'William, we need to have some fun because we've been here eight hours, why don't we go out for dinner, and we just have a more social time.' So, we did that several times and, of course, when you do that, just like in the business world, you talk about a lot of the business you've been doing but you also ask about each other's families and you also tell them a story about something you were doing the previous week and some funny recollections of previous meetings. That is an important part of diplomacy."

What is a leader without their followers? Someone taking a walk. Like all of the business applications of humour that we're exploring in this book, the essence of leadership can be found within a human relationship. What is it that inspires one person to follow another?

Mark Bedford, bass player with the ska pop band Madness, says, "Anyone who can make people laugh or share their humour is always invited in. If you get that cooperation of people on your side, and invariably you form a better relationship, and maybe in the context of business, you can get things done a bit more."

A leader needs a vision, yes, but more than that, they need a team. Maybe we could define an entrepreneur as a leader without a team, but in reality, everyone relies on others to get things done. Even the person who declares themselves 'self made' needed customers, suppliers, investors, lawyers and accountants, and in order to scale any business they will need staff. There is no such thing as a 'self made' man or woman, only one who claims to have done it all themselves. In the corporate world, organisations often reorganise and restructure, and people and teams are moved around. You might start a new job working for one manager and then in six months' time, find yourself in a different team with a different manager. You might apply for a transfer or internal promotion. You might formally recognise the authority of your line manager, but you wouldn't automatically describe that person as a leader. 'Manager' is a function, a job title. It describes a relationship, but that relationship operates on more of a transactional. To recognise someone as a leader is a very different matter. You cannot be made to follow a leader. You can begrudgingly accept a change in your role or your working conditions, and you can take on an undesirable task or project whilst muttering under your breath if you feel that you have 'no choice'. You could even feel threatened with losing your job. If you've ever worked in such an environment, you'll know that your level of engagement and commitment was as low as possible whilst still keeping your job. In such situations, people 'work to rule', they withdraw their discretionary effort, they do the minimum in order to keep their jobs. They are not happy and they are not productive.

The highest performing businesses in terms of employee engagement achieve 22% greater profits than those with lower engagement, and businesses that develop the strengths of their staff have been shown to reduce staff turnover by up to 72%[5]. Staff loyalty impacts on both productivity and profit, and is critically dependent on the quality of leadership within the organisation.

A leader who engages and supports his or her team will turn resentment into responsibility. People will be willing to take on undesirable tasks and projects because they know that they are supporting their team, and that their team mates would do the same for them, and they know that the leader of the team will roll up their sleeves and help out too. There is a clear sense that 'we are in this together' and humour is a vital tool for the leader to achieve this.

Comedian and broadcaster Matt Forde says, "If you look at the success of Boris Johnson, in particular, he really proves that having a sense of humour is part of persuading people to vote for them. But if you look at quite a few of the successful leaders in my lifetime, Tony Blair was very funny, David Cameron was pretty funny. It's not the most important thing. But humour is the single best way to make people warm to you as a politician, or as a person in an office environment. If someone's funny, they tend to be one of the most popular people in the office. Equally, people who think they're funny and aren't are often amongst the least popular. For politicians to be able to show that they can laugh at themselves, that's a huge asset. A lot of them can't laugh at themselves, particularly not at the time when it would be most advantageous. A lot of them can look back afterwards and be quite funny. At the time, they find it very difficult. Finding that sweet spot shows a level of self awareness. They have to be an authority figure, they have to be serious, they have to be trusted, but also we want to know a little bit about them and we want to feel some sort of connection with them. That's important, not just in getting people to vote for them but also for those people who don't vote for them. Just that sense that I lost but I can live with that person being in charge. That's why leaders' speeches always have a few jokes in and they are often terrible. Humour is a weapon particularly at Prime Minister's Question Time where the single most prized asset is that punch line put down, augmented now by the ability to go viral on social media. It is probably more important now than it's ever been."

Perhaps there is a symbiotic relationship between the leader and their court jester, and one cannot function effectively without the other.

John O'Farrell isn't just an author, scriptwriter, and political campaigner, he understands the vital role of court jester very well, having been a lead writer for some of the UK's greatest satirical shows in recent years, *Spitting Image* and *Have I Got News for You*.

"It's harder to do a show like that today. First of all, back in the 1980s when *Spitting Image* came along, there were four channels and *Spitting Image* was viewed by millions and millions of people. Now the audience is scattered much more widely across hundreds of channels, so you don't get that shared national experience that you had back then. The other thing I would say about that time was that, believe it or not, our politicians were still held with a certain amount of reverence and our royal family were held with a certain amount of reverence so there was a pedestal to pull them down from. Now, with Donald Trump or Boris Johnson, I don't really think there's anything that you could put in their mouths that would be more ridiculous than what they're saying already. So how do you satirise people who are light entertainment performers already? That's what got them elected. It's a much harder job to prick that pomposity when it's already a comic persona that's been elected to office.

With Donald Trump, his public persona was invented on The Apprentice in America, he pretended to be a top businessman when he'd never been a particularly successful businessman, his fortune was inherited and he managed to not lose all of it. Yet there's this fiction that he was this top, hard hitting businessman. With Boris Johnson, he pretends to be a bumbling, jovial buffoon, and sells it as a brand and it's a breath of fresh air to some people, as a contrast for the boring, cautious, suited businessmen that we've had.

Humour is a highly valuable asset for anyone in politics or business and to have a good joke at the top of a speech gets the audience on your side and it relaxes them. The most successful politicians do know how to woo a crowd and that includes being funny, Obama was funny, Tony Blair could tell a joke. To be capable of engaging an audience, a good sense of humour is something that should be in your armoury. That said, Mrs. Thatcher had a terrible sense of humour, she could never tell a joke, and that never did her any harm."

Culture

"Humour… that's how you unite people."

Ainsley Harriott

Dan Snow sums up the importance of humour in creating culture. "Hunter gatherer societies still exist in some small parts of the world and anthropologists have been studying them since the 19th century. We know that humour is one of the mechanisms that we use to cement group ethos, ideology, build teams, build relationships."

Film director and comedy writer Guy Jenkin thinks that humour can actually be used as a health indicator of an organisation's culture. "A friend of mine was in a marketing meeting with Amazon and there were about 50 people on the Amazon side of it. So his opening remark was, 'So who's delivering all the parcels today?' which I find very funny, but apparently went down like a lead balloon. You could probably judge the health of one of those companies by going into it and seeing whether people are laughing with each other. Feeling unfettered, when they're working towards an idea or being able to go off on some tangent that is funny, and actually may lead somewhere. It makes people want to come into work."

Humour can transform the most mundane job. Laughter makes time fly. After all, you have fun on holiday and it's gone in a flash, whereas boring meetings at work just seem to drag on and on. Surely, there's a lesson to be learned from this?

Comedian and TV presenter Tony Robinson talks about his experience of filming a new TV series. "I'm going into oil refineries, the docks, servicing the ferries, all the big jobs that people do through the night that we don't know anything about. It's like listening to a comedy show all the time. It's not because they're psychotic, it's not because they're unlike anybody else. It's that they can create an atmosphere where they can at best enjoy what they do, and it works better when they do."

Having fun at work isn't just about building stronger, more productive teams. People want to feel fairly rewarded at work, which means that they want to feel that their contribution is recognised and worthwhile. Many managers worry that this means they have to pay more money for bonuses and rewards schemes, but financial incentives have been shown to actually demotivate people in the long term.

An experiment with 21 fast-food retailers found that when managers used non-financial incentives, profits increased by 30 to 40% and, after six months, increased productivity and profitability to the same extent as the financial incentives to which they were compared[6]. Non-financial incentives can take many forms, and of the simplest is to simply get your team together and have some fun. It probably wouldn't be as effective to put a group of disgruntled colleagues in a room and order them to have fun, so of course you have to bear in mind the normal working environment too.

Research published in the Journal of Vocational Behavior in 2016 showed that fun at work "has the ability to improve employee resilience and optimism, which leads to better attention to tasks. Fun also has the potential to bring co-workers together, which can foster learning among colleagues."[7]

The research also found:

- Fun activities were significantly related to overall informal learning
- Manager support for fun was significantly related to learning from oneself
- Fun activities were significantly related to learning from others and non-interpersonal sources

The team that plays together not only stays together, it also learns together and succeeds together.

Many studies have demonstrated a clear link between employee engagement and performance, with organisations in the highest quartile for employee engagement seeing 41% less absenteeism and 22% higher profits than those in the lowest quartile.

One of the interesting questions in the 2016 Eurofound[8] research was "Time flies when I am working". 76% of people from across 35 European countries agreed that time did fly when they are working, most or all of the time and you know what the old adage says about time flying - that it flies when you're having fun. Groucho Marx also noted that "Time flies like an arrow, fruit flies like a banana", which I think you'll agree, further emphasises the point.

Work engagement has been described as a 'positive, fulfilling, work-related state of mind that is characterized by vigour, dedication and absorption' (Schaufeli and Salanova, 2007). The opposite, according to Maslach and Jackson (1981) carries the signs of burnout: exhaustion and cynicism. I would venture that cynicism is a good way to describe the opposite of humour.

Cally Beaton makes an important point about psychological safety, an aspect of team dynamics which Google[9] found was the single most important common factor in all of the high performing teams that they investigated in 2012. "One of the things that's very topical at the moment in companies, if we look at what younger workforces want, it's all about balance and well being and having their voices heard and telling their stories, and about being able to stand out, not having to fit a mould. You've got to create psychological safety and humour is a really important way to allow people to be vulnerable. Leaders in businesses will definitely engender more trust and safety in their employees if they can also show chinks in the armour and so a quick way to show vulnerability without baring your whole soul is humour."

John O'Farrell brings together Cally Beaton's thoughts on responding to the changing needs of a younger workforce with Marcus Brigstocke's advice, to always be nice, to always begin by complimenting people.

"Barry Cryer was on the TV quiz show *Pointless*. Alexander Armstrong said to him, 'When was the golden age of comedy?' and Barry had the best answer you could give, which was, 'We're living in the golden age of comedy. There's so much talent around, there are so many brilliant new comics coming up and it's a pleasure to still be doing it after all these decades.' That's the answer I aspire to give, to stay relevant, to stay interested, and to keep learning from people younger and fresher than you."

It's so easy to blame problems on the last boss or the next boss, the last government or the next government, the last generation or the next generation. Barry Cryer's warmth breaks down those divisions and recognises and obvious truth; that we're all in it together.

The good leader uses their humour to build a positive, supportive, enjoyable and fun workplace in which people can do their best, feel that they are treated fairly, pull together, solve problems, overcome challenges and most of all, go home at the end of the day and say to their partners, "Something funny happened at work today".

Political heavyweight Alastair Campbell was the voice of the British government for 10 years through the 1990s and early 2000s. He led teams through some very challenging times, creating a strategy for communicating with the nation and the world. He says, "The key to business success is a happy and healthy workforce who are prepared to be innovative and think differently. You're going to get happier, healthier, more innovative workflows if you encourage people to enjoy themselves."

International cricketer Ebony Rainford-Brent has faced her fair share of cultural challenges as the first black woman to play for the England cricket team. "I've been in environments where it's not okay to be yourself and you have to fit the image of what the leader, the coach or the captain says. When you have a good leader, they let people be free to be themselves and that allows them to flow more and have an environment which supports difference and diversity. To get to that flow state, to get to those performance states, you need to be being as close to yourself as possible. You need to be as relaxed as possible. It's about the leader creating a good environment."

It doesn't have to be the manager that makes the working environment fun, anyone can do it. Founding member of the comedy musical group Fascinating Aida, Dillie Keane, remembers her time spent in a series of boring office jobs. "Laughter is a great lubricant. I worked in offices for many years, because I didn't enter showbiz until I was 26. I worked at an advertising agency, in various lawyers offices and things like that, in a secretarial capacity, and I worked in bars and of course in bars, you can have a joke with people, but in an office it's fairly dull. I remember fleeing the headquarters of William Hill, because this guy kept coming in and saying 'Well, roll on Friday!' and he said it all Monday, and by Tuesday morning, I'd had enough and I just walked out. I couldn't face it. Because if you're there all week saying 'roll on Friday', that's misery. Whereas you can look forward to working and have a laugh with people and get down to work. I remember I was working in a company that made blinds and I had such a good laugh at the women on the opposite side (of the office) because I was typing the invoices. Now I'm a very fast typer and I would do three quarters of an hour really hard, just ferocious typing and then I'd go, 'right I'm taking quarter of an hour off' because I'd start getting things wrong. I'd crack jokes and things like we'd have a bit of a laugh around the office and they would be hugely amused, so I said, right, I'm going to send an invoice every 70 seconds. I was partly doing it because it was a very dull job, and it made light in the office. It was fun."

You will no doubt have heard the phrase 'the war for talent', which is based on the idea that smart people are 'out there', not within the organisation already, and that employers have to compete for the best people. Often, this results in employers creating cool, trendy workplaces which look impressive but which can hide toxic working practices. Cricket commentator and former England team captain David Gower agrees. "If you're trying to build a business it's not just about putting a ping pong table on the side or funny pictures on the walls, it's about creating an environment where someone comes to work thinking, 'I want to see John, Sarah, Reggie, Julie, because they're good people, we work well together and we get the job done.' Anyone who has spent time in a dressing room knows that the interactions between players are absolutely vital. Tension needs deflecting and there are all sorts of situations which needs humour. Humour unites people."

Culture can create a sense of belonging. If a new hire is joining a business, we could argue that it's the responsibility of managers to induct that person into the culture. This would be wonderful in an ideal world, however in many large organisations, the new hire is often left to fend for themselves. On one hand, you hired them, you should look after them. On the other hand, you hired them for their experience, they should hit the ground running.

The important point is that, whilst your new employer perhaps *should* help you to settle in, you might also want to make it easier for yourself.

Ainsley Harriott's early life was influenced by just such a desire from his parents. "My parents were immigrants and they wanted to be accepted. We went to the local church because it meant that you became part of the community, you get to know local people. We weren't the only ones. I'm talking about a whole cross section of people from different parts of the world that were not necessarily associated with Church of England but in order to be able to settle in, to assimilate, that's what we did. When your parents bring you up like that, then you learn to make people feel comfortable accepting you, they are not afraid. I'm saying, I'm not going to threaten you, I'm smiling with you and making you feel good. Then sooner or later, we're having a cup of tea chatting. It served me well worldwide, from the early 1990s of travelling globally, making all these TV programmes, meeting fascinating people that speak a completely different language, but hey, the smile and the food are universal. It just brings people together, you're sharing, it's the breaking of the bread, sipping the wine, sharing the same vessel and stuff like that. All those things, that's how people come together. That's how you unite people. Our family found a way to bond people and to smile and make people happy."

Simply, if you want to be accepted into a culture, start by making people smile.

One aspect of culture which is vitally important but has perhaps been overlooked until recent years is equality, diversity and inclusion. You might argue that this is three aspects, but they do tend to stick together.

It's easy to think that there is no place for humour in such a sensitive, political and potentially inflammatory subject, however, think about humour's role in levelling playing fields and bridging divisions. In particular, think about the role of satire in breaking the glass ceiling of the establishment.

Yasmin Alibhai-Brown is journalist, author and regular commentator on issues of immigration, diversity, and multiculturalism. "When I became a journalist, which was very late in life, I was 37 and I woke up one morning and became a journalist. Literally I wrote an article. I couldn't type – a week later, it was published in *The Guardian*. Very soon after that, I had a very rapid climb up the ladder and at one point an editor from a liberal, shall we say, 'left persuasion' got a bit drunk at a media party. He lurched over to me and he said, 'Oh, you've really done well. Of course it was the Brown that made the difference. You wouldn't have got this far with that foreign name, would you?' So I looked at him with my glass in my hand and smiled and said, 'Yeah, I know I was so lucky to find him, but imagine where I'd be if I'd married a Mr. White!' There was a group of people all around us and they just fell about laughing, and there was a lesson in racism that he will never forget."

Yasmin goes on to demonstrate that she's not afraid to use humour to say what needs to be said, even in the most confrontational of situations. Her power doesn't come from status, it comes from her willingness to say what other people are afraid to.

"I was born without any fear of position, so I can laugh. I can laugh at anyone who's got power because to me they're the same as anyone else. I don't believe in the hierarchy of human beings. I don't believe some people are born to be given such respect that we may not laugh at them. If you are a believer in equality, then you absolutely should be able to bring down or laugh at everyone, including yourself. As my mother used to say, just imagine them sitting on the toilet and then you won't be afraid.

When Boris Johnson was foreign secretary, we were all going on the Andrew Neil show. We were in the chairs outside the studios in Millbank and another sex scandal had just broken with him. I said to him, "Mr. Johnson, I'm really upset with you." He knew me because we'd been on a couple of foreign trips, so he said, "Yeah, well, what, what?" I said, "I'm the only woman, it seems, who's not been asked by you to have an affair with you. I'm incredibly upset!" Everybody fell about laughing, and he went red with anger. He was not pleased. He was not pleased. He didn't laugh along with it."

Tessy Ojo reflects on humour as a more personal way of dealing with life's challenges.

"I see humour more as as the best medicine. You could spend all of your time thinking about the things that are wrong, or you could also find space to be grateful for the things that that are. I always think about gratitude as my default attitude in that sense, and humour allows me to see the beauty of life. Sometimes you see the ugly side of life, the inequalities, the disadvantages, all of the ills in society, but every now and again, you really have to sandwich all of that with thankfulness, with a grateful heart and just find the beauty that's in life."

Within an organisation, you can create the culture exactly as you want it to be. Culture isn't in the walls or the furniture, it's in how people connect with each other. It's entirely possible to create a culture that brings people together, that offers a better way of working, that focuses on the beauty that's in life.

Arthur Smith sums it up rather nicely. "Humour is what brings us together wherever you are in the world. Every country, every human, has some element of humour. Even if your skin colour's different or you speak a different language, humour can still bring you together."

Sales

"And I'll throw in my pet frog"

Karen O'Quin and Joel Aronoff

As I mentioned in the introduction to this book, customers rarely buy the best of anything, because there are so many variables that it's often impossible to quantify the best option. Instead, people will buy what feels safe and what they feel subjectively attracted to. In turn, they will feel attracted to what makes them feel good, and smiling definitely makes them feel good. In 2011, researchers at the Face Research Laboratory at the University of Aberdeen, Scotland[10], asked people to rate smiling and attractiveness. They found that both men and women were more attracted to images of people who made eye contact and smiled than those who did not. That should come as no surprise. What you might find more interesting is research into what can cause a smile.

The part of your brain that is responsible for smiling sits in the cingulate cortex, an unconscious automatic response area. In a Swedish study, people were shown pictures of faces expressing a number of emotions. When the picture of someone smiling was presented, the researchers asked the test subjects to frown. They discovered that the test subjects' natural inclination was to smile, and they found it very difficult to consciously frown. If you want someone to feel happy, get them to smile, and if you want them to smile, smile at them.

Studies even show that something as simple as adding a playful line to a sales pitch, such as "My final offer is X and I'll throw in my pet frog" can increase customers' willingness to pay[11] by 18%. A Christmas cracker joke can actually raise your value.

Add this to Robert Cialdini's[12] work on influence, which found that one of the six critical factors in influence is 'liking' and you have a simple, powerful, all-purpose recipe for success in sales - smile.

As if I need to spell this out for you, if you want to sell more, and you want your customers to be 18% more likely to buy from you, and you could achieve that simply by smiling and approaching your work with good humour, then why wouldn't you do that?

Let's compare sales with dating. Both are massive global industries. Both involve strangers deciding to work together to achieve some mutual benefit. Both are based on trust. Both conclude with celebratory posts on social media. Oh, and of course, in both cases, the more you actually like the other person, the better it turns out for all involved.

In a 2021 research study[13], psychologists found that people were very capable of assessing the intelligence of another person, but that this perceived intelligence was not the reason for choosing a potential mate.

"Self-reported mate preferences suggest intelligence is valued across cultures, consistent with the idea that human intelligence evolved as a sexually selected trait. The validity of self-reports has been questioned though, so it remains unclear whether objectively assessed intelligence is indeed attractive. In Study 1, 88 target men had their intelligence measured and based on short video clips were rated on intelligence, funniness, physical attractiveness and mate appeal by 179 women. In Study 2, participants took part in 2 to 5 speed-dating sessions in which their intelligence was measured and they rated each other's intelligence, funniness, and mate appeal. Measured intelligence did not predict increased mate appeal in either study, whereas perceived intelligence and funniness did."

In plain English, the researchers measured intelligence and then compared this with attractiveness, to find that people who were smart but not funny were not attractive, but people who were funny were attractive. Funny and smart were most attractive of all. Funny brings people together, smart can push people apart if there's an element of superiority to it. Therefore, if you have a choice of how to present yourself to a potential partner or a potential customer, choose funny over smart.

One aspect which is vital in any relationship, not least in sales, is trust. Trust is a prediction about the future, the knowledge that a certain person will act in a certain way, and ideally in your best interests. You much prefer people who are reliable. Even though unpredictable people can be fun, they can also be tiring.

In 2021, Dr Magdalena Rychlowska from Queen's University, Belfast, investigated three different types of smiles and how they can influence social judgments and trust in situations where there could be conflict.

The smiles which represented reward, dominance and affiliation are a little different to each other. A reward smile is encouraging and shows that a person is happy, whilst a dominance smile reinforces status. An affiliation smile builds social bonds and says, "we're in it together".

Dr Rychlowska's study with more than 900 participants looked at how people reacted to reward, dominance, and affiliation smiles after being badly treated by a competitor during a game. She says, "Facial expressions are very important in building social relationships and not all smiles are an expression of joy."

"We found that when a person smiled after being uncooperative or untrustworthy, they were viewed as being happy and therefore they appeared untrustworthy and unwilling to change their behaviour. However, when an affiliation smile was used, this was perceived as an attempt to make amends, restoring higher levels of trust than the other two smiles."

It turns out that we don't just respond to any old smile, we also consider the type of smile and the context before choosing to trust someone.

You can smile, and you can offer your pet frog into the deal, but your product or service still has to meet the buyer's needs. Nowhere is this perhaps more evident than in the world of business investments. If you buy something that turns out to not do what you thought it would do, you take it back, you get your money back, everyone's back where they started. However, if you're investing in someone's business then you are taking a huge risk because you could lose all of your money if the business doesn't perform. Business investors therefore have to understand not only the commercial viability of the business but also get to know the people they're investing in. Deborah Meaden, one of the longest serving investors on TV's *Dragon's Den*, says, "We've had some real fun in the den with people who have walked away with no deal at all. Laughter creates a bridge, it creates an atmosphere. Once they've got the dragons laughing, they're more likely to be able to get their message across. Laughter plays a part, but we're dragons, we're not just going to invest because we find somebody funny."

Based on this, you can imagine that if an investor has a choice over the businesses they invest in then they might lean towards the business partners that they can enjoy working with. Certainly, there have been numerous instances in *Dragon's Den* when the dragons invested in the person, not in their business idea.

Any investor or business owner knows that a product or service can be amazing but it doesn't sell itself. Some form of sales team has to go out and represent a brand, whether through direct sales or indirect sales through a retailer. If a sales person genuinely enjoys their job and loves the thing they're selling, you can expect that enthusiasm to rub off on the customer.

Deborah Meaden goes on to say, "I invest in businesses and I would expect them to know a lot more about those businesses. They're living, eating, breathing, sleeping them. My job really isn't to know it at that depth. It's to know enough to sort out who knows what, so that I can pull on expertise to help me help them so I shouldn't know the intricacies of a business I should know enough to make sure that when they ask me about the big stuff that I can actually add value. If I went in with the big 'I know everything', I would probably cause a lot of business failures because I don't know everything. So people who enjoy their work are good at their work, they're good at it because they want to be at work and they go out as great advocates and in a world where you're trying to attract a really good workforce, you can have an army of people going out saying that it's a fantastic place to work, I enjoy my work, I have fun. We know there are the serious moments but there are the fun moments too. So it's really, really simple. People who enjoy their work are good at it, and they stay."

In almost every sales environment, market forces ensure that the customer has a choice. All things being equal, a customer could buy any product that solves their problem. They could buy any mobile phone, any car, any brand of clothing. In practice, people have preferences and strong allegiances to brands, and those allegiances are of course created by marketing experts who know how to influence our emotional responses. From a marketing point of view, it doesn't really matter why we remember something, it only matters that we do remember it, and that we remember it the next time we're buying. Rick Wilson, political and media consultant and founder of The Lincoln Project, says, "We had to do things that had inherent humour and virality to them. And the virality, it could come from either being funny and witty, and cutting and weird, or it could come from being emotionally resonant and powerful."

Going viral is of course one step up from being merely memorable because when a marketing message 'goes viral' it is passed from one person to another, usually through the immediacy of social media. It seems that being weird or resonant could take a lot of hard work and research, whereas being funny could be equally effective and much easier to achieve.

Presenting

"Be nice."

Marcus Brigstocke

Once again, I will refer you to my esteemed tome *The Pitching Bible* for a lengthy and yet entertaining journey through the world of pitching, which I have defined through The Seven Secrets of a Successful Pitch. However, there is an even simpler truth which you must know to achieve real success in your pitches and presentations - be liked.

That's easy to say, but very hard to achieve because it's not under your control. You might have experienced what happens when you try to get someone to like you, only to achieve the opposite.

Comedian Marcus Brigstocke has good advice to share, that the easiest way to be liked is to be nice to people. "It's easier than everyone thinks. Lots of people come to me for help with writing a best man's speech. I've got to deliver a best man speech, what should I do? What should I do? What do you want to do? They'll always tell you the same thing, 'I thought I'd get up and call the groom a bit of a twit. Then I'd mention the time he crashed his car.' I give them the same advice every time. I say get up at the beginning of your speech and tell the audience how much you love the groom. Tell them this is my dear, dear friend, and he's asked me to be his best man. I am so happy to see him here today, doing this beautiful thing, marrying someone who he loves who I'm coming to know and who I love. It makes me so happy.

Right? That audience will allow that best man to be the least funny human on Earth. It couldn't matter less.

So the advice is simple. Be nice. Be nice. I'm not always nice on stage, but I am when I first come on stage, I'm filled with a genuine love and gratitude for the people who have come to see my show. If in business you have to deliver some sort of speech, and you think there's some expectation or requirement that you might have to be funny, be nice first, because if they don't like you, from your first few comments, you'll never get it back. If you get up and you think it's fine, because you know Janet, who's introduced you, she's head of HR and you go way back and she wears the most awful shoes, and you get up and you go, 'Thank you, Janet, and I must say, what an appalling pair of shoes.' Well, as far as the rest of the audience are concerned, they've just seen a man say something really unkind to someone who they quite liked, and they don't know the context. So don't do it. Don't fall for the trap that slagging people off is going to make you popular. Be nice first."

John O'Farrell certainly agrees with the advice to be nice to people first. "Make jokes about yourself, or about the boss that they're all exasperated by, don't put down some poor secretaries sitting in the front row, or just going up to get a drink. Self awareness and tone are the key things if you're going to be doing a joke at a serious event."

Danny Wallace explains the importance of humour to punctuate communication. "That the best communicators that I've seen always throw some humour in no matter what they're talking about. Audiences sometimes need that little release. If you're talking about something very heavy, if you're talking about something that makes people uncomfortable, it's quite nice just to punctuate it with a little moment that lets everyone breathe and go, Okay, good. We're allowed to make a noise. Now we can concentrate again."

Perhaps the most common use of humour in presenting is in the 'ice breaker'. A fear of public speaking is the most common fear that people experience, more common than a fear of death. I've died on stage a few times, so I'm certainly past worrying about that one. When a person is afraid of speaking in front of an audience, they are generally afraid of what they imagine is going to happen. What I've found is that many people say that the first few minutes are awful, but once they get started they relax and it's not so bad. What this tells us is that, almost always, people who are afraid of presenting are afraid of the start of their presentations, not the end. In order to overcome their nerves, they turn to the cliché of the ice breaker, a terrible joke told to break down the barrier between the presenter and the audience.

Maybe you have seen presenters using such ice breakers and maybe you have found yourself responding in the same three ways each time:

1. Cringe at the awful joke

2. Cringe at the presenter's nervous delivery

3. Wonder what on Earth the joke has to do with their presentation subject

I personally advise against using ice breakers, for a reason that is so simple that you won't believe me.

My advice is that you don't use an ice breaker because…

There isn't any ice to break.

When you use what can be recognised as an ice breaker, you are signalling to the audience that they should feel distant from you, uncomfortable, detached.

The ridiculously simple fact is that you didn't just wander in off the street and start lecturing people. The audience is present because they know what's happening, they have an idea of what to expect and they are already willing to listen and pay attention. There is no need to break the ice. They are not strangers.

For your presentation to have its maximum impact, it must be consistent. No personal small talk. No comparison of golf handicaps or football results. No enquiries about the wife, weekend or future holiday plans. As Marcus Brigstocke so perfectly summed it up, "Be nice first, because if they don't like you, from your first few comments, you'll never get it back."

Your ice breaking joke is most likely irrelevant. It has nothing to do with your presentation. You might get a laugh, but then you have to deal with the discomfort of changing the subject. Your audience likes you because you're telling a nice joke. They want you to carry on being the comedian. They don't want to hear about sales figures.

I'm sure you've seen this in action. "And the barman says, you can come in but the guy in the monkey suit has to stay outside! Anyway... um... but seriously... so I'm very excited to introduce our new product the Flangemaster 2000 which as you can all see comes in two very eye catching finishes..."

If you want to introduce your pitch with humour, start easy. Use personal experiences, oddities, irony. The more personal, the more universal. Let the audience laugh at you, not at themselves, and certainly not at the person sitting next to them. Humour has to be inclusive, not divisive.

Avoid telling jokes unless you're selling your services as a stand up comedian. This has nothing to do with your ability to tell jokes, it is because telling jokes and then moving into a business pitch breaks rapport. By opening with a joke, you establish your role as that of entertainer, not as business partner. Let the jokes come later.

There is a place for levity and lightness but the very best presenters simply allow humour to flow from the situation if and when it is appropriate. Here's a wonderful piece of advice from John O'Farrell, from the time that he was writing scripts for the satirical TV show *Have I Got News For You,* which illustrates that spontaneous humour has the advantage of being relevant to the moment.

"Angus Deaton was presenting and Paul Merton would interrupt my hilarious joke with something funnier, and I would just sit at home really frustrated. I did a brilliant joke for that, I can't believe it's not making it into the show. But my jokes on that show were really a safety net in case nobody said anything funny. That was fun to be part of such a great show, but not the most satisfying sort of writing when most of your stuff ends up on the cutting room floor. But again, you've just got to accept that's the gig and deal with it."

I've seen situations where the person chairing the event had to get their jokes in, even though they're not really necessary. Think of your jokes as a safety net and allow other people the space to be funny too.

Perhaps the most important outcome of any presentation is that you are memorable. You're unlikely to change the world for the better if people can't remember you or your message. William Hague has spent a lifetime speaking publicly, for entertainment at one end of the scale and to win votes at the other. "If you want to hold an audience's attention, you have to get them to do things because of course, faced with one person talking continuously, people's minds drift off. The human brain didn't evolve to just sit around the campfire listening to the same person for an hour. So therefore, if you're going to impose a long monologue, you do have to liven it up for them to keep them engaged. Now that can be anything from getting them to applaud or to cheer, or to cry. I find that the best way of doing that is to get them to laugh, that re-engages them, gives them some connection with the speaker, and it gets their attention back. I often tell people, if they're going up to be selected as a parliamentary candidate, for instance, and they've just got 10 minutes to give a speech to a group of people they've never seen before to get them to vote for them, I say to make sure that every 90 seconds, you get that audience to do something. It might be to laugh, it might be to clap, but they will remember you. They've got to try to remember 10 different people who appeared before them for 10 minutes. If you get them to do something every 90 seconds, they will remember you."

Some people struggle with larger audiences, saying that they're happy to present to one or two people at a table but get nervous when they have to stand up in front of many people. However, this may actually be counter-productive. Magician, comedian, presenter and writer Paul Zenon offers an interesting insight, saying, "If I watch comedy on TV, it's seldom I laugh out loud, even if I find it funny. Whereas if I'm in an audience, I'm more likely to vocalise it, because I'm letting everybody else know that I find it funny. Being part of an audience is an interesting psychology." When you present to only one or two people, you're relying on them to do all the work to keep the energy flowing. When you've got a larger audience, they will be communicating with each other as well as back to you. Paul goes on to say something that many of the Humourology podcast guests have noted, "A comedian needs to hear a roomful of people laugh at once. The problem with something like Zoom, is you can't hear the laughter coming through apart from one person at a time."

Cally Beaton makes an important point too; that individuals behave differently to groups. "The way in which whole groups of people listen, as opposed to individuals, is very different. When you're looking at a sea of 3,000 faces and you think they look blank then yes, that would be a blank look if you were having a coffee with that one person, but you're not. So they may well be listening but not feeling the need to emote what they're feeling."

This raises an important point about a phenomena that psychologists call 'social proof'. In the context of humour, you're more likely to laugh if someone else is laughing, hence the 'canned laughter' used in many TV sitcoms and even in the theatre, where professional 'claquers' were employed to applaud enthusiastically.

Of course, for the social aspect of audience participation to work, you do need an audience. Journalist, politician, former executive editor of The Times and member of the House of Lords Danny Finkelstein recalls the time when even the most enthusiastic of claquers would probably not have helped.

"I went once to give a speech in Norwich. From where I live, it takes something in the region of five hours to get to Norwich University, you have to get to the train station, wait for the train, it takes several hours to get there. I was giving a voluntary speech, I was not being paid. I open the door and there are literally two people and one of them is the person who had invited me. What do I do? I thought I'd better give him a talk, so I sit down and I do a slightly embarrassed version of what I was supposed to say anyway. At the end of it, I said, 'Would you like to join the Young Social Democrats?' and he said, well, I would, but it would interfere with the terms of my parole. Then I had to stack all the chairs and go home again, five hours.'

Danny Wallace notes that the effect of social proof can work, not just for laughter but for any emotional response. "It's like a virus. It's like going into an office and just sneezing all over everybody. Scientists have found that even witnessing a moment of rudeness is enough to turn you much ruder as well, because something has been triggered in your mind. Even now, the fact that I am saying, imagine something rude has happened, it's like I'm grazing the skin because people listening will be thinking about rude events that have happened to them or real events that they have witnessed and it makes you angry and it also confuses you, because it goes against what we all agree society should be. So when we see someone being rude, they're breaking the rules, and we are confused, we can't work out why it's happened. If it's happened to us, we're immediately riled up and the chain of rudeness happens because you then take that rudeness home with you and you're perhaps a little shorter with your partner. Maybe you don't sleep as well, maybe you drink more. The next day, you're much more likely to leap straight to rudeness yourself."

Perhaps the most important advice from Paul Zenon is that making a connection with your audience doesn't have to be complicated. It doesn't have to involve ice breakers or jokes or complicated methods of building rapport. The basic foundation of any human interaction is eye contact, so simply begin by actually looking at your audience. "I met a legend, Sir Ken Dodd. He was just lovely, his stagecraft was incredible. I noticed the first time I ever saw him when I was about 10, that within 15 to 30 seconds of walking on stage, he made eye contact with everybody."

Of course, your power to control your confidence begins long before you're in a position to make eye contact with your audience. People who are nervous of public speaking don't begin to get nervous when they stand up to speak, they get nervous when they imagine standing up to speak. Have you noticed that?

It simply comes down to the ideas that you create in your own head when you imagine your presentation.

TV presenter and singer Katrine Moholt becomes aware of the words in her mind. "It's all about being properly prepared for what you're doing and not thinking, 'Oh, my God, now a million people are watching me and now we're going live.' If you're starting to have these bad voices in your head, then you're lost. The better I am prepared, the more I'm prepared for the unprepared. I have done *Strictly Come Dancing* for 10 years and it's live. Every Saturday, I ask myself, 'Why do I do this?' but then I go in front of the camera and the nerves are disappearing because I focus on what I'm going to do."

Simply, be conscious of what you're saying to yourself. It's unlikely to be true. One great piece of advice that I've heard is to actually talk back to the internal voice. When you hear criticism, judgement or fear, reply by saying, "Thank you, and what do you suggest I do differently?"

Either the fear disappears, or you get some useful, actionable advice, both of which are big improvements.

Cally Beaton talks about mental movies instead of words. "I used to have a real fear of public speaking, I was absolutely terrified of presenting in anything more than a boardroom setting with a few people around a table. I did have to learn to do it but I didn't feel as if I would be a natural at it. You can play a couple of different movies in your head. If the movie you play in your head is messing up your words, the audience hating you, falling over on the way to the stage, wishing you'd never done it, then there's a chance that might happen. Choose to play a different movie in your head before you go on."

If you want to present confidently, simply make that the movie in your head.

Networking

"Life is too short to spend time with people that don't bring you joy."

David McCourt

In my book *The Pitching Bible*, I share a detailed system for how to excel at building your professional network. I won't repeat myself by sharing it here, what I will share is the very simple observation that when you think about who you might know who you can recommend for something, you don't necessarily think of the person who would be best, you think of the person who is most memorable.

David McCourt puts it perfectly, "Life is too short to spend time with people that don't bring you joy. People who don't give you energy, people who don't make your life more fulfilling. There are people that suck energy out of you and there are people that give you energy, and you find yourself wanting to spend time with people who give you energy. So people are going to perceive you that same way. If you spend time with someone, and they feel better after after they've done spending time with you, they're going to want to spend more time with you. If they feel exhausted after spending time with you and they feel drained, they're going to want to spend less time with you. So you want to deal with people who give you energy and make you feel good. Certain people walk into a room and you just smile. Before they say anything. You just smile. You want to be around them because they make you feel good. Life is too short to spend time with anybody other than people like that. You want to spend time with people who love doing things you love. End of story. Game won."

You might be wondering how you can be the person that others want to spend time with, and again, that's far too complicated, and if you try to be what other's want, that's definitely a recipe for your own unhappiness. Instead, you simply begin by spending time with the people you enjoy being around. The rest will flow from there.

Arthur Smith advises, "There is a saying that laughter is the shortest distance between two people. That's true. Because if you meet somebody, you don't speak their language, but you both laugh over something, then you have a connection. Humour is something that will always bring people together."

The Pet Shop Boys hit *Being boring* was inspired by a quote from American socialite Zelda Fitzgerald about whom was said, "she refused to be bored chiefly because she wasn't boring".

Therefore, if you don't want to bore other people then don't be boring. Easier said than done? Then try this. Don't talk about subjects that you're not interested in.

Katrine Moholt advises, "Only say yes to things that you're passionate about, then it comes easily, because you love what you do."

Find the subjects that inspire you, that make you light up, and talk about those instead. Do you think that anyone goes to a networking event to hear interesting stories? They go to meet people. Telling stories just gives you something to do while you're making connections. How do you want your new connections to remember you? Knowledgeable but boring, or interesting and friendly?

Networking involves meeting new people by finding common ground, and we all enjoy being around 'like-minded' people. How do you attract people who are like you? Simply by being yourself. I know, you hear that a lot. You should be yourself, everyone else is taken. But how can you be yourself if you don't know who that is?

The search for identity is a huge global business, paying the salaries of everyone from self-styled self-help life coaches to remote mountaintop gurus and shamans. Well, you can't figure out who you are by looking inward. The answers are outside of you, an in particular in the way in which you interact with the world. You judge the personality of other people by noticing how they act and react, but you can't see your own reactions until other people point them out. Therefore, other people tell you what your personality is, and what's wrong with it. "You're so arrogant!" or "You're very kind" or "You listen to other people too much!" or "You never listen!"

These comments say nothing about your personality, they only reveal the speaker's expectations of you. How other people judge your reactions is largely irrelevant as long as you're not going out of your way to be awkward and annoying. What this reveals is that your actions are what influence the outside world, not your thoughts and hopes.

As you look around you right now, you see the results of your previous actions. You see the 'stuff' the you have accumulated in your life. You see the letters, photos, notes, mementos which are important to you. If you didn't throw it away then you made a choice to keep it, and that choice reflects something about you. So if you want to know what you're like in order to know what constitutes like-minded people, simply look around you. You have surrounded yourself with evidence of what you do, what you enjoy and, most importantly for our purposes, what amuses you.

When you try to be what you think other people want you to be, you will surely end up dissatisfied. When you seek out the life experiences which you enjoy, you will attract other people who enjoy the same experiences. People gravitate towards each other.

Comedian, writer, producer, television presenter and, according to *The Observer*, one of the 50 funniest people in Britain, Jimmy Mulville says, "Humour is a fantastic key to open doors because if I come in and tell you how brilliant I am, and all the great shows that I've done, the drawbridge comes up. Then you start being defensive and you start thinking that I'm here to tell you how great I am. If I come in and say about a shit morning where this, this, and this happened, we can have a laugh about it. Then what are we? We're both human beings trying to make sense of our lives."

If you go to a networking event with a 'scarcity' mindset then you are more likely to be pushed into trying to be like other people. If you think that you desperately need to make a new contact or find a new client then your actions will reveal your desperation and you are unlikely to make a good impression. If you consider that this is only one networking event of many, and the right people are out there, and they would be drawn to you if only they knew you were there, then it gets much easier to 'be yourself'. Rick Wilson says, "If you have some authenticity, and an engagement with what's really happening around you, you're going to be funnier, you're going to be more valuable and engaging than you will be otherwise."

I'm sure that you've had the experience of being at a party, conference or wedding and feeling bored with your group's conversation. As you hear the raucous laughter from another table, you think to yourself, "I wish I was sitting over there". If that happens to you at every event you go to, you might start to wonder if there's a common factor at your table's lack of mirth. Remember that laughter is a social signal, telling other people to relax. If you're laughing, you're letting other people know that you're safe to be around. Except, maybe, if you're laughing for no obvious reason in the style of a mad scientist or maniacal despot. Let me start that again. If you're laughing appropriately and at the same time as the other people in your group, you're letting other people know that you're safe to be around.

To put it simply, if you want to meet like-minded people, then let them see the real you through your humour. Sure, some will warm to it, some won't, and the result is that you'll always attract the people who are right for you.

Interviewing

"A joke signals that you have a sense of humanity, a sense of humour, and you get it that you're not a superhuman. That's a social lubricant."

John Sweeney

If you're attending a job interview, I suggest that you do two things. First, read my book *Pitch Up!* Second, invest time in thinking about what makes you memorable.

Does this mean that you leap into the interview with a spinning bow tie and jokes about the office furniture? Well... no. However, it's natural to feel anxious during an interview and humour, as you have discovered, is a natural way to release the tension that could otherwise negatively affect your performance.

Comedian and impressionist Alistair McGowan says, "There are some people who have a glint in their eye who will engage in some wit and exchange and others who just don't. Life is always better when people are able to have a bit of fun. What's the difference between being nice to people and being funny? Being nice means you're being warm, you're being considerate, you're probably being quite witty with them."

TV producer James Longman gives another important insight into how to use humour to relax in an interview, "Everyone's got the ability to be funny. You meet people along the way who are unintentionally funny and make you laugh. People work better, and work harder, if you've got humour in your life and in your work and everything. You're happier and lighter. If you're in a happy place, it's easier to focus and it's easier to get on with what you need to, without worrying about other things. Laughter and comedy helps you get into a better place."

James raises an important point – that you don't only need to use humour within the interview itself, you can actually use humour privately in order to relax yourself before you get in there. When you're on your way to the interview, make a point of looking out for things that make you smile. Jokes, funny adverts, signs that you can interpret in an amusing way, unusual situations and people can all help you to reset your emotional state and walk into the interview in that happier, lighter state that James described.

Robert Cialdini's book, *Influence: Science and Practice* cites a great deal of research into likeability. For example, people are more likely to give you something if they like you. Whilst that might sound obvious, there's a big difference between what we think we know and what can be proven through experimental significance. It means that it isn't only you and your friends who experience something, it means that this is common to all human beings.

In an interview, or in any social situation, how do you get someone to like you? Remember Marcus Brigstocke's words, "Be nice first, because if they don't like you, from your first few comments, you'll never get it back."

It's easy to think that when you go into a job interview, it's their job to put you at ease. They're interviewing you, on their territory. They ask the questions. They call the shots. If you're nervous, it's their fault.

Consider the alternative. They're making a huge decision as the result of this interview. They are committing to an investment in whoever gets the job. In a very short space of time they have to get enough information about your entire career history to make the right choice, to get the right person on board. That's a huge personal risk for them. The wrong choice can cost their company a lot of money, it can destroy teams and damage customer relationships. If you were to get married, would you just pick the first person you see on a dating app? Of course not, you get to know them first, you have to make sure they're right for you because the consequences of failure are expensive and damaging.

Paul Zenon emphasises the fact that people value humour and will relate that personal value to business value. "It's no great coincidence that when people go on dating apps quite often they'll put GSOH which normally is an indicator that they don't have one. They put bubbly when what they actually mean is bloody irritating. But it shows that it's a valued trait in human beings. A valued trait in a relationship, like a sense of humour is equally valued in business, it's why people like other people, and if you like someone, you're more likely to buy from them." More likely to buy from them, and more likely to hire them. Who wouldn't hire someone who is fun to have around the office? Someone who makes life easier for their colleagues?

When someone is hired into a job and they turn out to be an appalling choice who lied in their application and clearly has no clue what they're doing, who gets the blame? The interviewer, for not doing their research, for not asking the right questions for not picking up on the obvious clues.

Now imagine that it's your job to put the interviewer at ease. You can let them know that they made the right decision in talking to you. You can let them know that their personal reputation is in safe hands. You can show them that you are a likeable person.

Maybe you don't get the job but I guarantee you'll be remembered, and I've seen many instances where the candidate was asked back to interview for a different role because they were "such a good fit for the team". Because they were liked.

Negotiating

"There's a deal made. If you come and see my show, I must make you laugh."

Marcus Brigstocke

"He made humor a tool of diplomacy. His banter inspired banter in others and usually led to a more relaxed atmosphere in the private, formal discussions or negotiations with world leaders. The humor opened the door to more frankness and less ritualized recitations as well. In that regard, Kissinger lightened the whole heavy international diplomatic scene."[14]

If Dr Henry Kissinger can use humour in the serious, life or death negotiations of international politics then there's no reason for you not to manoeuvre a modicum of mirth into your work.

As the United States National Security Advisor and then the Secretary of State during the time of intense global mistrust and impending nuclear holocaust known as the Cold War, Henry Kissinger used his sense of humour to great effect at the negotiating table[15]. Such a respected statesman probably didn't tell jokes for the sake of being funny, or to be the life and soul of the party, but instead because he knew that the right humour, at the right moment, could move the discussion along and open up new possibilities.

One interesting piece of research into the use of humour in negotiation had test subjects discussing the price of a piece of art[16]. The seller was, secretly, one of the researchers. At a certain point in the negotiation, the seller made a 'final offer' which required varying degrees of concession from the buyer. The final offer was either presented as-is, or was accompanied with a joke; "and I'll throw in my pet frog."

The size of the concession made an insignificant difference to the agreement reached, which shouldn't be surprising since no-one actually knows what art is supposed to cost anyway. In fact, no-one knows what anything is supposed to cost, other than by believing the people who set prices for things. Money is just an idea, a concept which relies on mutual agreement.

Regardless of whether the seller demanded a small, medium, or large concession, the buyer reached an agreement more often with the joke than without it. Perhaps, at the right moment, the humour diffused the tension caused by the mismatch of expectations, and by diverting that emotional energy into the joke, the focus was taken away from the required concession.

Perhaps a moment of laughter also creates a social bond. If we're on the same side, we must already agree with each other, right? If we're on the same side, then your price must be fair because people who agree don't take advantage of each other. Logically, you know that this doesn't hold true, but emotionally, we are hard wired to trust people who are like us, and shared laughter is one of the best ways to gauge that.

That social bonding also allows the buyer and seller to retain their composure and dignity - to 'save face'. "Face-saving reflects people's need to reconcile the stand taken in a negotiation or an agreement with their existing principles and with their past words and deeds."[17].

Sports agent and former Leicester City chairman Jon Holmes has negotiated some of the biggest deals in British sport and for him humour is just one of many ways that he can achieve a win-win outcome. "There's no one way. The idea that something is the answer in negotiation is not true. It's all the circumstances where you are at the time. I've negotiated for a living for ages and ages. Did I use humour in it sometimes? Yeah. Did I sometimes play the hard man? Yeah. Sometimes. There's no good way to do it, it's what's appropriate in the circumstance. It's looking at the guy on the other side of the table and working out how to do it. If someone's on your wavelength, if they're talking to you and you get a point of contact, it does work. Sometimes that involves humour, sometimes it doesn't. Sometimes you're keener to get one step ahead of them. Sometimes you withhold certain information. Sometimes the best way to do it is to actually be completely open. But it's all about the dynamic of the relationship in order to achieve where you're going. Power and humour are ways of getting people on side."

Self-deprecating humour could also cause the person on the other side of the negotiation to shift their position in your favour. You've seen this work countless times in personal relationships. The offer of "This dress/suit makes me look fat" receives the counter-offer of "You look wonderful, darling!" Did you ever think of such a discussion as a negotiation? Even the legal term for this, an "invitation to treat", tells you all you need to know!

Marcus Brigstocke talks about the contract which is negotiated between the performer and the audience as a set of rules that determine how each person behaves. "Comedy is a transaction. I do funny thing, you laugh, right? If you're not laughing, I'm not doing my job. I really like how straightforward and measurable it is as an art form. So when I'm developing a new show and I'm trying new material that I know isn't ready yet, that contract between me and the audience isn't yet formed, we're still negotiating. When my show is ready to take on tour, I then have a contract with you. If you're not laughing, I'm not doing my job."

Coaching

"If I can make you laugh first then you're going to engage."

Dani Klein Modisett

Coaching deals with the thorny subject of personal change. I say 'thorny' because the client's journey of self discovery often begins with an external event or some feedback which suggests that their life is not all that it could or should be. Even the client who says that they want to achieve more out of life often has a nagging doubt that, somehow, their life is less. If the coach dives straight in with a critical analysis of what's wrong then a negative, remedial tone has been set. Coaching is easy when it's all goal setting and awesome empowerment. The real test of a coach is when the going gets tough.

The coach who approaches every conversation and situation with equal good humour achieves something so much more important than lightening the mood of the coaching session. To do so would risk trivialising the client's experiences. Instead, the coach who is an adept Humourologist offers the client what they need most in order to move forwards; acceptance and perspective.

There are coaches who specialise in laughter, an approach which itself is an offshoot of laughter therapy, the idea of which is that laughter releases endorphins which increase a person's tolerance to pain and reduce stress, resulting in better resistance to illness and improved recovery.

Often, the concept of coaching is associated with achieving the highest levels of performance in a particular field. The rapid growth in the coaching market in recent years began with sports coaching and in particular the field of sport psychology. The idea was simple; the human body has physical limits but the mind does not. We can only make an athlete fitter or stronger to a certain degree, limited by their DNA, but their mind is a limitless source of potential. If we could somehow tap into the power of the mind then we might be able to achieve higher levels of performance in a sport. We can say that two athletes of similar physical size and strength should perform similarly but, in practice, their performance flows from their mindset. The coaching industry today is largely derived from this way of thinking, that it's a high achiever's mindset that separates you from the average person, not your body or your upbringing.

Penny Mallory is an award winning author, TV presenter, a keynote speaker, performance coach, and former rally champion, who is now an authority on mental toughness. She was the first woman to drive a world rally car at world championship level. However, her life hasn't always been a smooth ride. As a child, she saw alcoholism and mental illness destroy her family. Fleeing home at 14, homeless and fending for herself on the London streets, her life couldn't have been more bleak. Yet an inner strength enabled her to take control of her future.

"You have to be able to laugh at yourself, because part of elite performance is, and I don't like the word selfish, but it's about having a really clear, laser focus on what you're trying to achieve. If you focus on one thing, all your time and attention goes to achieving that thing, everything else will be not attended to. That would appear to be a selfish approach, but you don't get to the top of anything with any other approach. Really, it is so demanding, and it requires so much of you. But obviously, if you can laugh at yourself, whilst you have that approach, it's extremely helpful, you can be such an utter pain in the ass to everyone around you when you are an elite performer, trying to put everything into one mission, you can become really difficult to be around. So maintaining humour, being able to laugh at yourself and what's going on is really important."

Penny's comments on humour once again emphasise a point which many of my interviewees have made, that it's not a one man, or a one woman show. Everyone needs a team, and maintaining a good relationship with your team through humour is vital to your success.

One important aspect of coaching, and of course its siblings mentoring, counselling and therapy, is listening. If the coach isn't listening to the client then they're following an off-the-shelf formula, they're not interacting.

Michael Fenton Stevens raises an interesting point about listening and timing, which is a similar idea to that shared by many of my guests, about finding the right moment for a humorous interjection. "Practise letting people finish their sentences, let them get to the end. Don't jump in on them. Let them say what they're going to say and if you hear something you want to comment on, put it in your head, and save it. Then you can come back to it, you don't have to do it at that moment."

Comedian and actress Dani Klein Modisett says, "I wrote a book about marriage and laughter called 'Take my spouse, please'. It's a great book because chapter two is listen. As a comedian, you learn that the audience is your scene partner. So if you're not working off what you're getting, then everyone feels that the moment is not truthful and they get distracted. So for example, I have my setlist, and then the waitress comes forward and drops a tray of drinks at the foot of the stage, but I'm so committed to my material that I'm not gonna react. But meanwhile, the whole audience is seeing that, the energy has changed, there's something's going on in the moment. So if you're not in that moment, you've missed an opportunity and that is translatable to all relationships, if you're unable to be present to the moment to really take the person in. Listening isn't just with your ears, it's active listening, body language, tone of voice, words, the whole enchilada. That comes right out of stand up, to be able to listen in that way to take in the whole energy in the room, whether it's one on one, or a large audience, it's absolutely essential."

Listening, then, isn't just about gathering information. It's about joining the other person in a moment of truth, a moment of honesty about what's happening. According to Katrine Moholt, "If you are a really good listener and laugher, you will be welcomed in every company. That's what people want, somebody who understands."

One of things that coaches often get asked to do is to have 'difficult conversations'. This presents an interesting paradox. On one hand, as Cally Beaton says, "Be careful when you use humour as a way of masking things that actually matter, for example if you can't say something real about yourself without self deprecating or having a bit of a gag about it." On the other hand, humour can be used to introduce a subject that could be too challenging to dive right into.

Steve Richards is a writer and presenter of the show *Rock 'n' Roll Politics* which uses humour to engage people in a subject which could certainly be seen as challenging. "It's amazing how much humour creeps into it, because when you are exploring these characters and their flaws, and the dramas that are wrapped around them, of which they have to be pretend to be in control, but they are not. You have humour, because on one level, it is absurd. That is the fundamental absurdity, that the government have to pretend to be in control of everything, when they're not in control of very much at all. I did a live show where the other two speakers were Esther Rantzen, talking about television and her glittering TV career and Martin Bell talking about his time as a war correspondent. I thought that no-one was going to come to hear about whatever was going on in politics at the time. Actually, I found they loved it but you've got to draw them in. If people are passionate about football, I can get them passionate about politics, because it's the same reasons for being interested, you don't quite know what's going to happen next to your team. You don't know what's going to happen next in politics, the ups and downs and personal dramas."

Dani Klein Modisett recalls a show that she wrote and performed that worked in exactly this way. "*Two Thin* was a comedy show about eating disorders, about anorexia and bulimia. We told funny monologues and we went to every college in the United States. The fact that we were honest, and had a sense of humour about our personal experience opened the door. It's saying, yeah, this is the truth and it's okay to talk about it. When my father died, I was doing another show called *The Move*, which was about giving up my apartment in New York to get married. The story was about grief but I couldn't just say 'Oh, here's a play about grief, everyone'. I played a crazy, funny single woman who didn't want to get married, who was afraid to get married, but then three quarters of the way into the show, when you're already laughing and you're with me, then we see my father's sweaters that I won't throw out, and that I won't go out the door. I will not leave the apartment. It was all a setup for a conversation about how we grieve. If I can make you laugh first then you're going to engage."

It's very hard to reach someone if they can't listen to you. Humour might offer you just one way to bridge the gap, to make a connection that could then lead to greater and more powerful insights.

Learning

"The best teachers at school were the ones who entertained us."

Neil Mullarkey

Neil Mullarkey, a comedian best known for his improvisational work at London's Comedy Store and in TV's *Whose Line is it Anyway?* now works with organisations, using his comedy and improv skills to teach professionals to be more flexible and resilient in their communication.

"It's well established that if you're laughing, you're going to learn stuff. If you're not laughing, you're going to be a little bit antagonistic. You might not be engaged. The best teachers at school were the ones who entertained us. Sometimes we were laughing, sometimes we're intrigued or asked questions, they give demonstrations that brought us in. I find that a lot of people don't like corporate training. But if I can say, actually, I'm making you laugh, there's a bit of learning here as well, that's why I really believe that, especially in my world of improv, you can learn something from it while having a laugh. Not only do I believe that you can learn while laughing but the laughing should be part of our everyday life. It's one of my great beliefs that we're all kind of a little paradox. My children think I'm very serious and then I'm very silly, I'm deeply embarrassing and then I'm very bossy. We can all allow ourselves to be a bit of both. That's what I liked, the learn and laugh thing. Many people who know what I do say that I get around the side by making them laugh and then bring in something more reflective, but never too far from a moment of humour."

Comedian and star of TV's sketch show *The Fast Show* Arabella Weir connects laughter with learning through the memorable nature of fun. "If I were spending money on me, I'd want empirical evidence that learning through teaching people lightness of touch and joy means they actually deliver on the message. I would back it up with an example, such as 100 people were taught Dostoyevsky and can't remember the lead characters names, but 100 people were taught Dostoyevsky as acted out in a fun way by comedians and acrobats and they remember the whole plot. People who are engaged and entertained won't necessarily say 'Oh, I laughed myself sick' but they absorb the information, they take it away, they retain it.

You've only got to see a man screaming at you out of his van because you indicated the wrong way to think, that guy must not ever have known what it is to say, 'I'm really looking forward to work today, I'm going to talk to my great colleagues, I'm going to get in my van which I love, I can't wait to deliver stuff'. You remember every time someone's been pleasant in the supermarket or the delivery guy's been charming. He doesn't even have to say good evening, he doesn't have to be obsequious. He just has to respond with lightness. Engaging with people in a human and light way makes people feel better and it makes them want to go to work and be loyal to their jobs. What is life without enjoyment of work? When that delivery driver comes and they're kind and helpful and you respond kindly, think how much better life is for everyone. Showing people that enjoyment in what they do through humour is an absolute goldmine."

Self-help guru Dr Richard Bandler has devoted much of his life to the study of how humans learn and change. "I'm kind of in the entertainment business. They force people to go to school and bore them to death for years and then wonder why they don't learn that much. If you don't make learning feel good, people don't do it on purpose, it's only possible when you can create an environment where people are having fun. It's easy because most people, if you really listen to what they're saying, you can find the nonsense in it. Sometimes I just say really ridiculous things and if if you can't laugh at yourself, you can't move on. Einstein was accosted by somebody at Princeton, they came up and they said, 'I'm so glad to be at Princeton, I heard that you teach here?' He said, 'No, I don't teach here. There's far too much teaching and not enough education.' She asked him, 'Well, can you explain to me just something about the universe?' He said, 'Yes, it gives us everything.' If you look at the universe that way, and realise that we're not in it, we are both apart from and a part of it, from the beginning of time until now, we're all made out of the same cosmic stuff. The limits in what we can understand are only the limits in what we can understand. They're not the limits in what's possible."

Even the world's most famous entertainer of all, Walt Disney agreed; "I would rather entertain and hope that people learned something than educate people and hope they were entertained."

Team building

"We have an innate desire to fit in. Making people laugh is one of the greatest things you can do."

Alistair McGowan

Many professional comedians have turned to corporate team building for a very good reason - laughter bonds people.

International Rugby star and my colleague on Sky TV's *School of Hard Knocks* Scott Quinnell has spent a career building teams. "You need a shared common goal to start with. You all need to understand where you're going. You all need to understand what you need to achieve. Whether it's a sports team, whether it's business, whether you're just working in a small group or a group of 1000 people. If we don't know where we're all going, what's the point in doing what you doing? Humour brings a lot into that, especially if you're together locked in sport, you'll be travelling a lot. You spend a lot of time in a changing room. As a professional athlete, it's not the amount of time you train, it's the amount of time that you get to rest and recuperate and have the wonderful facilities in and around you; the ice baths, the cryotherapy chambers. If you don't have the humour in and around this, there was one guy there with us in the Scarlets and his name was Ian Boothby and he was a brilliant openside forward. He is a brilliant man and he brought the humour to it, every week somebody would have their trainers or their shoes or after the game, you'd be going to get changed and he'd tie your shoes up or put them in the freezer, in an ice bucket in the freezer. You'd come out and there your shoes were, frozen, and everybody would have a giggle over that. Apart from if they were your shoes! He would bring quizzes on buses and aeroplanes and everybody would just have a laugh and get engaged. It was a common thread throughout the squad, and he was the catalyst for that.

The important thing with humour is the fact that when you're struggling or when the team is struggling, because when things are going well, everyone's on cloud nine, but when you're struggling, that's when you need somebody just to pick you up, somebody just to say something that breaks that silence puts everything in perspective. Once you're able to do that, you can discuss what's happening and you can get on with it. Everybody gets down and so a lot of the time you go back to the old adage, a problem shared is a problem halved. People do that a lot through humour. Somebody just says one thing that could change your mindset, or push you in a different direction."

It seems that good team work depends on good humour because within that sense of shared purpose is a deeper sense of 'we are all in this together', and humour is such a simple and powerful way to do that. A strong team develops its own culture, and within that culture the team even has its own sense of humour, its 'in jokes'. Many business leaders and entrepreneurs have told me that their one priority is to make sure their team feel so good about working there that they never want to go anywhere else, and even in large corporate organisations, managers have said that they want a team spirit that makes other people want to move into their team. Central to all of this is the amount of time the team spends having fun. That doesn't mean playing practical jokes like in Scott Quinnell's story, it means giving each other the energy to get through the tough days, because then the easy days take care of themselves.

Perhaps you've experienced office humour going too far, or taking precedence over work, which can be equally frustrating as talk show host Clive Bull describes. "I have been in one or two workplaces over the years where it's all been a bit too jokey and I haven't actually liked that. You've got to be serious about the job but do it in a good humoured way. There's a very delicate balance and it's a really skilled boss who creates a nice relaxed atmosphere but you focus on the job at the same time. If you get the right atmosphere then people will want to work more. I've had some very, very funny bosses over the years. Some who are not cracking jokes all the time but they do things with a wry smile or twinkle in the eye and especially when you're working with a lot of younger people, a lot of producers and reporters coming up through the ranks, it needs to be an enjoyable experience. It's a very delicate balance, you can see when it works and you can see when it doesn't. If people are just living in fear then that doesn't work."

A low level of daily conflict will erode trust in the strongest of relationships. When personal relationships suffer after years of sniping and put-downs, imagine the impact on office relationships, where the people involved 'just work there' and don't need to invest time and energy into getting along with each other. The stress caused by a toxic working environment is immense, and ultimately, team building isn't about getting people to have fun, it's about getting people to communicate with each other in order to resolve the conflict which inevitably arises when a group of people are working on common goals in an environment where resources are limited.

Professor Sophie Scott is the Director for the Institute of Cognitive Neuroscience at University College London and she has been doing some very innovative research into laughter[18].

"There's a really lovely set of studies from Robert Levinson in the US, where he's been doing a longitudinal study of married couples. He gets the married couples together and he puts them in a stressful situation. He asks one member of the couple, 'Tell me something that your partner does that irritates you'. Just run that one around your head for a second! What he found is that couples find that stressful. Imagine doing that. You feel stress. It's unpleasant. You can measure that physiologically – heart rate changes, galvanic skin response, which is a measure of sweat, that changes. It's a stressful thing to do. What he finds however, is that couples who deal with that unpleasant, stressful feeling with what he calls 'positive emotion', things like laughter and smiling, not only immediately get less stressed, but they're also the couples that are more likely to stay together for longer and are happier in their relationship. It's not because laughter is like a little bit of magic dust that makes everything okay. It seems to be because it matters if both members of the couple laugh. If one person laughs and the other person doesn't laugh – you know one person's saying 'Oh it is actually quite irritating, I can imagine, that I snore so much every night' and the first person is saying, 'it's a massive problem, and I wish you'd stop.' No one feels better. No one feels less stressed. The laughter only works if you laugh together."

Let's dwell on that last point for a moment. "The laughter only works if you laugh together". I could not have put it any better. In an office environment, it's common that cliques and silos form, in which people tend to form like-minded groups that create a sense of belonging and safety if you're in the group, and alienation if you're not. This social grouping behaviour starts very early on in life, it extends through school and through your working life. One of the goals of team building is therefore to break down the barriers between these groups and restore trust. As Sophie puts it, the laughter only works if everyone laughs together. Since humour is a powerful tool for social inclusion, it's also a powerful tool for social exclusion, when used maliciously. I imagine that, at some point in your life, you have experienced that - as most of us have.

Another point worth noting from Professor Scott's work is the importance of dealing with stress in teams. When there's conflict of disharmony in a team, stress is the result. On the other hand, when a team is unified by laughter, they can deal with any amount of pressure without it turning into stress because they know that they are all working to achieve the same goals. Stress doesn't only come from life or death situations, it arises at any time when people feel pulled in different directions or pushed to behave in ways that they are not morally comfortable with. Host of the *Down To Business* talk show Bobby Kerr recalls, "I remember working in kitchens, working in very pressurised situations. Humour really is the greatest tonic when you're under pressure. The place could be falling apart. Well, if there's a bit of banter going on, it actually holds all of them together. That's always been my way of operating."

One of the easiest ways to unite disparate groups is to create a shared challenge. A common enemy, if you like. Think back to what Alistair McGowan said, "I've been surprised sometimes doing corporate events where the head of the organisation will introduce me after they've made quite a lengthy speech, and that's always great fun because, if they've got a doable voice, you've only got to give a representation of it, a replication of it and people love it because you're doing the boss. Obviously you're respectful to him, but he doesn't have the status that he does for the staff."

An after-dinner speaker can unite an audience by making jokes about the big boss, or the evil competitor, or some other bête noire. When everyone laughs together, they must be like-minded, they must share the same story, walk the same path, have the same needs. They must be 'insiders'. You don't have to be a professional entertainer to have the same impact, just as long as you remember to keep everyone laughing together.

It's worth remembering that opportunities in life don't always go to the obvious 'star players'. Sometimes, the brilliant technician or the amazing sales person works best as a lone wolf. All too often, they get promoted to lead a team, a task for which they turn out to be ill prepared. Sometimes, a leader will recognise your potential, not to do a job but to enable other people to do their jobs, to create an environment within which the whole team can excel.

Ainsley Harriott's career took an important turn when a restaurant manager saw potential, not only in his culinary skills but in his ability to bring people together.

"When I was cheffing in the hotels and restaurants, my team stayed with me for a couple of years because they enjoyed the atmosphere. My old boss Malcolm gave me early responsibility when a lot of restaurants didn't want a black head chef because it was just the way it was at the time. They didn't want someone with dark skin to be running an established restaurant. Malcolm made me sous chef, he gave me an opportunity, he gave me the belief in myself to be able to do it. He told me, I want you to create the team because it's all about having team spirit in the kitchen. It's not about your great cooking because you're working with each other a long time. If you're doing split duty, or they're eight in the morning, you finish at 2:30. In the afternoon, you come back at 5:30, finished 11 o'clock at night. You've got to have a good team spirit there. If you're happy, it's reflected in the food. My mother always said that the is food smiling, you're putting energy into something you enjoy. When someone's put love and attention into it, it's a real pleasure. It's why we love home cooking so much, because there's a lot of love that's gone into it and that is reflected in the kitchen. That's perfection. You're proud of it. You might do it fifty times a night but you're proud of it because that's what it's all about."

Build a team who are proud to do what they do.

Organisational change

"If we don't find our mistakes humorous, we get to repeat them over and over again."

Richard Bandler

Perhaps the biggest problem in organisational change, and even on a wider scale, political and social change, is communication. Messages get mixed, accusations of fake news abound, conspiracy theories spring up like weeds. I'm sure you've worked in an office with an active 'rumour mill' which produced inside information on anything from office romances to the latest merger, with the accompanying redundancies of course. The challenge for organisational leaders is in how to communicate the right information at the right times, and then in how to get the right information to stick, and not be subverted by far more interesting and intriguing rumours.

The journalist Jon Ronson spent much time researching conspiracy theories, producing a book and a TV documentary, *The Secret Rulers of the World*. You might know one of his other works, *The Men Who Stare at Goats* which was even turned into a Hollywood movie, so astonishing were the truths, half-truths and outright nonsense that he uncovered. In one scene in the TV documentary, he obtained the minutes of a meeting held by a secret society said to rule the world. He showed the lengthy document to the reporter and conspiracy theorist who has devoted time to 'outing' this evil group who turned through the pages of the clandestine tome to then announce, "I can't believe they've gone to the trouble of taking out everything they didn't want me to see."

Human belief is incredibly strong, and is not so easily influenced by mere evidence. It's just as well, really, because our entire sense of personal security is based on an absolute, unshakeable knowledge of how the world is. Almost everything that you know about the world you live in is completely made up. You chain together a sequence of distorted memories and call them a 'holiday' or a 'career' or a 'relationship', but those intangible groupings do not exist outside of your mind and your own interpretation of events.

The challenge for the leader wishing to create organisational change is in creating and recreating beliefs about the future which are just as unshakeable as your beliefs about your self, your friends, your family, your life, your loves and your own personal dreams.

Researchers at the University of Pennsylvania[19] found that "Young adults are more likely to recall and share information pertaining to politics and government policy if it is presented in a humorous, entertaining manner."

"Our findings show that humor stimulates activity in brain regions associated with social engagement, improves memory for political facts, and increases the tendency to share political information with others," says lead author Jason Coronel, Assistant Professor of Communication at OSU. "This is significant because entertainment-based media has become an important source of political news, especially for young adults. Our results suggest that humor can increase knowledge about politics."

Global politics and organisational politics are very similar, and one of the key aspects relating to communication is the need to prepare people for the future without causing the kind of knee-jerk reaction that leads to economic failure. The management of the flow of information is vital. People in organisations often complain that they are treated like 'mushrooms', in other words, kept in the dark and covered in shiitake mushrooms. At least I think that's what it means. However, there are often some very good reasons for leaders to keep news of impending change to themselves. In regulated industries, and in publicly listed corporations, revealing information that can affect the state of the market or the company's share price would result in legal action. It is very difficult for a leader to talk about options and possibilities without those musings being amplified by the rumour mill into looming certainties. The executive has no almost no choice but to form a closed community and only reveal information as and when they are certain as to the direction they're moving in. It may or may not be a sign of their Machiavellian nature, what's important is the way that other people in the organisation feel about the information which has been withheld.

Being honest about withholding information is at least better, and therefore more reassuring, than denying that any change is being discussed. In this day and age, with the speed of environmental, technological and social change, any successful organisation must have change at the top of every agenda. It would be suspicious if leaders were *not* talking about change. What really matters to people, "is how does it affect me?" and that is the question that most depends on trust, and we have already seen many times the impact that good humour has on trust in a relationship.

Organisational change programs often focus on what's wrong with a culture, what's missing, what's difficult. A new culture is chosen as the solution to all the problems of out of date products, changing market conditions and global political turmoil. Maybe leaders are afraid to say that their employees are lazy idiots, so they blame the culture, when the culture is simply the working environment created by people.

Changing culture isn't about posters promoting new organisational values. A friend of mine starts every regular business meeting with the same question, "Are we doing this because it's working, or are we doing it because we're doing it?" In this regard, changing an organisational culture is no different to changing a habit.

Comedian, writer and broadcaster Robin Ince expands on this point. "Every company is filled with people who do absolutely nothing. For example, in the arts industry, the two most important things are an audience and an act, that's what you need. This is surrounded by people who make more money than everyone else in there, yet they don't make anything. When you face up to humour in the workplace, you might have to face up to the fact that you possibly should be redundant.

I have an obsession with meetings. What if you don't need five meetings a day so you remove one meeting? Just watch an episode of *Man Down* or some Laurel and Hardy together, watch something in a room together where you all find out what you laugh at, bringing people together through laughter not through division.

I have a rule, which is that I don't do three meetings if nothing's happened after the first two meetings. When we're working on projects, if someone says, 'Can we have another meeting?' I say, 'Well, nothing's happened after the first two, so we don't need another meeting.'"

Dr Richard Bandler has spent most of his life developing tools to help people create change. "If people change the way they think it changes how they feel, and therefore it changes what they can do. The irony is they've been doing it their whole life but they get stuck in loops, because they learn too well. Some of the things we learn are utterly useless and stupid and people who continue to do them, number one, are unhappy and number two, lose money, they lose time. The currency of living is how you spend your moments. That's not just true in your personal life, that's immensely true in your business."

The currency of living is how you spend your moments. It sounds simple, yet if you spend more time on the moments that matter, you create change.

Creativity

"When people laugh they can have new ideas."

The Dalai Llama

Comedian Marcus Brigstocke likens creativity to magic, saying, "Where magic exists is where something occurs to you on stage that would not have occurred to you anywhere else. This happens, particularly in improv, where your brain does something extra. If you ask me to write a lot of the stuff that I've improvised on stage, I'm not sure I would ever arrive at it. But stuff happens. To me, it's genuinely a magic trick. It's genuinely something was conjured out of the air that didn't exist before that moment. I'm glad to say that despite being a comedian for 20 something years now, I remain absolutely enchanted by it still. I find it magical."

Rory Sutherland is vice chairman of Ogilvy UK and is an expert on consumer behaviour, trends and the influence of the internet. "I latched on to behavioural science because human behaviour, by which I mean the gulf between how we pretend to think, decide and act and how we really behave and act, is inherently comedic. It's funny, because everybody knows there is this discrepancy between the official rational explanation for our actions and what really lay behind them, the evolutionary or instinctive forces that truly drove them.

The official rational explanation for why we buy and use toothpaste would involve prevention of cavities, dental, health, etc. Yet, when you look at when people really clean their teeth, it's got nothing to do with this. Would you clean your teeth before a date? Almost certainly. Do you clean your teeth before sex? Do you clean your teeth first thing in the morning before you go to the office? Yes. Do you clean your teeth after lunch when it would really make sense? Almost never. It's much more driven by the vanity and fear of bad breath and by having gunky teeth than anything to do with long term dental health. Further evidence for this, the fact that 98% of the world's toothpaste is flavoured with mint. A lot of people don't even like mint, mint has no contribution to dental health, but it has a hell of a contribution to making your breath and mouth feel fresh of wholesome.

What's supposedly going on and what's really going on are not really correlated at all. That kind of thing is funny because it's the job of comedians to puncture the bubble of our own rationalist self delusions. Comedy does that remarkably well. That role of comedy in bursting assumptions is vital and it's possibly why we evolved a comedic instinct. Humour sits alongside music in that it's more or less common to all humanity."

Humour is therefore important in creativity because it provides a means to burst the bubble of existing assumptions, to overturn the status quo and see the familiar from a very different angle.

John Lloyd's television work includes *Not the Nine O'Clock News*, *The Hitchhiker's Guide to the Galaxy*, *Spitting Image*, *Blackadder* and *QI*. Early on in his career, he realised that everyone has an innate sense of creative intelligence, and the environment nurtures that.

"We are a company that essentially does comic things; podcasting, theatre, television, radio, books, our job is to make people laugh as well as make make them interested. So it's not surprising that there's a company meeting going on today, and people will be laughing a lot because they'll be talking about interesting, funny things. It's perhaps more difficult if you're making electrical fitments. My dad was in the Navy so we travelled all my childhood. The last thing I wanted to do with my gap year was go travelling, I wanted to earn some money so I got a job as a tea boy for a local builder called Mac. Eventually, they used to let me drive the minivan and pick up the cement. Then they taught me how to do plastering and tiling and it was the best job I've ever had, it's very satisfying that sort of craft work because you look back at the end of the day, the roof you've just built or the wall you've painted, and you think, 'We did that'. Then you go to the pub.

The guys were all much older than me, I was only 18. They were so funny, they were very good at their jobs. Nearly all of them were volunteer firemen in their spare time. They're all extremely bright and funny, we laughed all the time, and then they teased me rotten, because I was a long haired lefty. We all became very good friends. One of the things that makes me a reasonably good producer is that I like my audience. Perhaps they are working class people who didn't do well at school because they weren't taught properly. Their native intelligence, their problem solving gift is extraordinary. I lost every argument I had with these guys over lunch because they were very clever people. That's why I'm professor of ignorance.

The people who love *QI* are cab drivers and brickies who struggled at school because nobody understood that they thought in a different way to the standard way. They just soak up information. Black cab drivers have a part of their brain that's bigger than other people's. They're very, very bright guys. It's such a shame that we waste people's natural abilities, particularly because we're still teaching people as if we have an empire and you want to divide your cattle essentially into two kinds, the people who can process vast amounts of very dull information carefully and accurately, so they can become civil servants or bankers or corporate lawyers. Those are the people who get all the straight As and the other people who can mend things and drive trucks and push wheelbarrows around and are not required to think other than just do that. What we really need is more guitarists and more novelists and more creative people, more comedians."

Creativity isn't only about painting or music, of course. Human beings are innately creative in that we are natural problem solvers, able to think outside of the boundaries of the problem. This doesn't always come naturally, particularly when a team is 'stuck', and humour can be an excellent way to introduce a creative spark.

William Hague might not be the first person who springs to mind when you think about creativity, which makes his thoughts on the subject all the more interesting. "Humour has a big role in giving people perspective and allowing them to bond together. It's got a very big role in creativity. When I was preparing for Prime Minister's questions against Tony Blair, which I did hundreds of times, I used to have a team of people working with me, well known people such as Danny Finkelstein, George Osborne. A lot of the time we were actually coming up with humorous and ridiculous things that we couldn't really deploy at Prime Minister's questions. As Christmas was coming, we would say, we could ask Tony Blair does he believe in Santa Claus? Because if he says, yes, that headline will be 'man aged 48 still believes in Father Christmas' and if he says no, that headline will be 'Blair ruins Christmas for millions of children'. So we've got him, he can't say yes and he can't say no. Now, we couldn't really ask him without me looking ridiculous but it triggers a train of thought - what are all the other things we can ask him which are much more serious? Where he can't say yes, and he can't say no. We will have caught him, we'll have got him in a difficult situation on the floor of the House of Commons. So, to me, humour is very good at creating serious thoughts, it actually helps your brain on to other matters. It encourages lateral thinking, particularly when you're in a group of people.

Something that your mind naturally enjoys and takes part in actually helps everything to flow and so provided that humour is appropriate and it's not offending anyone, then it helps everybody in the room to take part in what's going on and gives them a connection with each other. There's no doubt about that."

A creative process is rarely an individual effort and perhaps the most important aspect of any effective team is equality, a sense that we're all in this together, and we're each as valuable as each other. Comedian and writer And Hamilton recalls his experience in writing for TV comedy shows where this was the case. "When I started out, there were a lot of shows where you were a paid contributor, but but you were in a room with lots of other paid contributors and you're all at different pay rates. It created a kind of wariness about sharing comic ideas, because you were effectively competing with each other. The money got in the way.

We did a show called Who Dares Wins on Channel 4. We had six writers and we put everyone on the same money. The writers room on that show was really productive because we were cross pollinating all the time. We had a massive engine of creativity and it fostered quite an adventurous approach, so we did some sketches that on other shows would probably have been ruled out as being too difficult. It gave us a sense of adventure and, and the fact that we were all in it together. One way of promoting creativity is to make everybody feel equally important.

There was a wonderful TV director, Liddy Oldroyd, who was a fantastic collaborator. If there was a problem, she would literally throw it open to the whole production team. She didn't care if the solution came from the runner who bought a coffee. She knew who everybody was, she knew their whole story. It meant that for the shows she worked on, the standard of problem solving was extremely high. Any creative process is going to involve an element of experimentation, so then the risk of failure will always be there. You have to allow failure but not be crushed by it. It's like in the improv world, where you listen, and you say, 'Yes, and', rather than, 'No, but'. If you've killed somebody's spirit, they're not going to pitch in with their next idea, which could be the brilliant one that saves the company."

What a lovely example from Andy; that we should always encourage an atmosphere of creativity because you just never know how brilliant your next idea will be.

Wellbeing

"It's no longer a question of staying healthy. It's a question of finding a sickness you like."

Jackie Mason

They say that laughter is the best medicine. I don't know who says that, but I suspect they're not shareholders of any pharmaceutical companies. However, doctors are well aware of the connection between good health and good humour.

Dr Phil Hammond, famous for his TV shows and books as well as stand up comedy with a medical angle, has professional experience of this. "Human beings are essentially social animals. We're like leaves on a tree and we want to belong. The best humour unites us. Humour can be very divisive, you can deliberately go out to upset and divide a room, or a patient and their relatives, but the best humour unites people. We very much need that, particularly at the moment. So the best communicating doctors I know have had very warm, compassionate senses of humour. But I've seen doctors who have no sense of humour at all, but who happen to be brilliant brain surgeons, and rely on their junior staff or the nurses to do the difficult communication for them. So there are lots of different skill sets you need to be a successful doctor. But in terms of the important stuff, most of health, interestingly, is built on relationships. If you look at what keeps people healthy over a lifetime, yes, there's luck, there's genetics, there's access to vaccines, etc. but actually, the healthiest people have strong relationships over the course of their lifetime that are built on love, compassion, and humour. If you have those three, you're pretty well set up for life."

Love, compassion and humour. I can't help you with the first two, not because I'm a psychopath but because they're not the subject of this book. Having said that, if I was a psychopath then I wouldn't help you anyway, so maybe there's no way to know for sure.

Luckily, Dr Phil has something to say about compassion too. "Comedy traditionally has a victim, whether you happen to slip on a banana skin or something terrible happens to you. A lot of comedians are now slightly frightened about addressing wider issues, because they fear upsetting someone. So the default position now for many comedians is to take the Mickey out of themselves. It's safe if you talk about my failings and my mistakes, which in essence, is what I've done over 30 years as a doctor and comedian, I go on stage and I talk about my mistakes. It's difficult because obviously, in medicine, if your mistakes are serious, then somebody may die as a result of it. So sometimes I had to sugar the story a bit. I've become much wiser and kinder and more compassionate over the years."

The message here about compassion is clear - it simply means that you take the time to think about the impact of what you're saying on the other person. Dr Phil performed in a double act at the Edinburgh fringe, telling some shocking stories about medical mistakes, and from that experience learned that what's funny to one person could be embarrassing, hurtful or frightening to another. Many jobs involve being the bearer of bad news, including doctors, HR professionals, engineers, lawyers and police officers. Knowing when to use humour to soften the impact, and knowing when to avoid humour is a fine and often difficult line to tread.

Wellbeing has become a huge strategic issue for business. For decades, business leaders have said, "people are our greatest asset", although I often felt that what they really meant was asset in terms of something that they own which loses value over time. Of course, what they really want their staff to think is that they are valued and cared for. Staff don't need to be told that, they need to experience that, and one way to do that is to care for their wellbeing. In recent years, more research has been done around the links between wellbeing, engagement and productivity and particularly since March 2020, wellbeing has been a major challenge for businesses worldwide because of the impact of social isolation and home working on the mental health of workers.

The ability to have sensitive, honest conversations with people in a business is critical to wellbeing and retention, and this is something that doctors have to do every day. Dr Phil has more to share with us on this subject.

"The medical interaction is a series of difficult conversations usually. Most of mine now are coming via video. I work in paediatric chronic fatigue. So I'm seeing young people with post viral fatigue, some had long COVID. We made the decision not to get let them go into hospital where there might be a risk they'll pick up another virus, so we do it all via video. There are lots of cues that you pick up when you're face to face with someone that you don't necessarily get remotely. In general practice, a lot of the consultations have been done on video, and they're less satisfying. Compassion is key in healthcare and just the gentle laying of a hand on somebody's shoulder or their arm can make a huge difference and you can't do that via a video link. But the bedside manner is still important. People remember kindness. If you've ever had bad news, you remember how it was broken to you and if it was done kindly, you never forget, if it was done harshly, you never forgive. Those moments really, really matter."

Dr Phil Hammond isn't the only doctor who has learned the importance of tickling the funny bone. Norman Cousins, the political writer published a book 'Anatomy of an Illness' in which he detailed his journey to recovery from a potentially fatal disease. He found that ten minutes of laughter gave him two hours of pain-free sleep which inspired a number of research projects.

Dr William F. Fry, a psychiatrist at Stanford University, California examined the physiological effects of laughter in the late 1960s and is considered the father of 'gelotology', the science of laughter. He showed that laughter can decrease your chances of respiratory infections and causes the body to produce endorphins which reduce pain and aid recovery.

Dr Lee Berk of the Loma Linda University Medical Centre studied the physical impact of laughter. Heart attack patients were divided into two groups: one half was placed under standard medical care while the other half watched humorous videos for thirty minutes each day.

After one year the 'humour' group had fewer arrhythmias, lower blood pressure, lower levels of stress hormones, and required lower doses of medication. The non-humour group had two and a half times more recurrent heart attacks than the humour group (50% vs. 20%).

Dr Hunter (Patch) Adams inspired millions of people by bringing laughter back into the medical setting with the idea that "healing should be a loving human interchange, not a business transaction". He is the founder and director of the Gesundheit Institute and has inspired the creation of thousands of therapeutic care clowns worldwide. You might know him from the film in which he was played by Robin Williams.

Dr Madan Kataria discovered that the body cannot differentiate between acted and genuine laughter. He then created a range of laughter exercises and techniques to stimulate this within a group. Laughter Yoga was born and is now known all over the world.

Researchers at Oxford University demonstrated in 2011[20] that continuous laughter increases people's pain threshold by as much as 10%. That might not sound like much, but it's a level of pain relief that drugs such as paracetamol might normally be prescribed for, leading to a holistic benefit for the patient and a cost saving for the healthcare provider.

In 2021, Scottish comedian and women's health physiotherapist Elaine Miller and Professor Helen Skouteris published their research into the connections between humour and health.[21]

Their review analysed 13 studies over the past 10 years in which humour had been used to communicate serious messages covering topics such as mental health, breast and testicular cancer self-examination, safe sex, skin cancer and binge drinking.

"What we found is that humour can act as an effective vehicle for delivering messages people might find fear-inducing or threatening. Humour, if used well, can be an emotional buffer that breaks down some of that fear so the underlying messages reach the intended audience and influence their behaviours and attitudes."

The study highlighted a number of factors that could impact the effectiveness of a humorous message, including the type of perceived threat, the 'taboo' nature of the topic and an individual's taste in humour.

"It's definitely not a one-size-fits-all approach. A poorly judged joke can ruin a health campaign's message, a therapeutic relationship, a gig; or all three of those at once. Humour is very complex and further research to examine humour and public health promotion is certainly warranted. What this study also highlighted is, there's a lot of us who work in health promotion who can learn from commercial advertising and public safety campaigns, such as road and rail safety where humour has been shown to attract attention, promote the memory of and positive attitudes towards an advertisement, brand or message."

I think you'll have to agree that whilst laughter might not be the 'best' medicine, it's certainly the most accessible and it's free!

Omid Djalili adds, "My parents took in sick Iranians who'd come over from Iran to Britain to get medical help. They found that if you kept the atmosphere light, if you made people laugh, they heal quicker. In Iran, the word for eggs can also double up as testicles. So they would say, 'how would you like your testicles this morning? Fried, boiled or scrambled?' It always made the guests laugh because they wanted to keep the turnover going. They wanted people to heal, so they got more people in. So it was actually a business decision that they used humour to heal people, get them out and get the new people in. It was actually a business decision."

So we have two fields converging; academics and doctors discovering the healing power of humour whilst comedians explore the humour potential of healing. Innovations can come in so many forms, as discovered by comedian and founder of Laughter on Call, Dani Klein Modisett. "I had moved my mother to Los Angeles from New York City where she was born and raised. She was a total New Yorker. She had Alzheimer's and she was depressed. She wasn't even leaving her apartment and it was $17,000 a month to keep her there so my sister and I decided that we would move her to Los Angeles to be near where I live, and the kids could visit and whatnot. Initially, she was OK but then realised she wasn't leaving, and she became depressed and withdrawn. I felt terrible. I felt really, really guilty. I was at my dentist and I was crying and she wasn't drilling. I said, I just feel terrible. I feel so bad for my mother. She's depressed and I just wish I could hire a comedian to cheer her up. She said, 'Oh, that's an interesting idea. Why don't you do that?'

The reason I had the idea was because I was a comedian and I couldn't make her laugh. When she looked at me, she saw daughter, and history and all that so I wanted someone fresh to come in with their sole purpose being to make her laugh. I put it up on Facebook that I'm looking for a comedian interested in a gerontology paid gig because I wanted somebody to respond and my phone rang almost immediately. It was Amy Stiller of the Meara family, very long term comedians in New York. She said, 'I just saw your post and I know someone in LA who wants to work with seniors. She likes sitting on park benches, you should call her.' So I call this woman and she came over and she did what we do now in the training. She understood instinctively that you get at eye level, and she was completely honest with my mother and didn't talk down to her. Of course, it helped that she had a New York accent. So she sat down and said, 'Yeah, I know. You don't want to talk to me. No, you're thinking 'Who is this schmuck just talking to me?"

There was something about the word schmuck that my mother liked so she said schmuck. The comedian, of course, said schmuck back. It was like this schmuck off. They were laughing and I just thought, oh, there it is. That's what I want right there. So I hired her on the spot to come eight hours a week to sit with my mother and to make her laugh. Within a very short time, it changed my mother's life, she opened up and even when the comedian wasn't with her, she was engaged with the community and she was eating again and it really changed her spirit. So I wrote an article about the experience for AARP magazine and I got hundreds of responses from around the world saying, please, can you bring a comedian to London? Absolutely. In Pittsburgh and Florida and Texas. That's when I said, oh, wait, I should really do this as a business because there's always comedians that need money and there's an endless supply of depressed seniors who could really use that kind of interaction. It was so effective."

We've all come through a period of great uncertainty, worry, anxiety. We've all been personally affected, in some way. In the darkest depths of lockdown, you might not have felt like laughing but now, looking back, you could consider all of the strange aspects of the experience and all of the things you did to keep busy, keep active or simply stay sane. When you share stories with your friends and your colleagues, you can choose to share stories of trauma and pain, or you can choose to lift their spirits with stories of hope and growth.

Kevin Cahill sums up the value of humour in supporting a healthy organisation. "If you're running a company or part of a senior management team, it's incumbent on you to try and create the culture and atmosphere where people can feel that they belong, where the achievements get celebrated, mentioned and talked about. Based on my own experience of running a large organisation, if humour can drive a sense of well being, then we can connect people."

We've seen, time and time again, that people are at their best when connected. Humour is a simple and powerful way to achieve that.

³Bouncing Back

"If you fail and learn from it, and you're funny, then it's all okay, everything will be okay."

James Longman

One area where the positive benefits of humour have been very well researched is resilience, the ability of a person to recover from setbacks in life. I learned this first hand during my time as a stand-up improvisational comedian at London's famous Comedy Store. When you're being roughly heckled late at night whilst standing on stage wearing a colourful shirt and straw hat, there's really nowhere to go. The audience at a comedy club can be tough, they can be uplifting, they can be welcoming but one thing they rarely are is forgiving.

James Longman, TV producer of shows such as *The Late Late Show with James Corden*, *Never Mind the Buzzcocks* and *Alan Carr: Chatty Man*, says, "You can fail and be funny. People just like you more, if you're funny and you mess up, then as long as you admit it and say, 'Oh, I messed up', people generally warm to you. It's easy to fail and failure is important. If you fail and learn from it, and you're funny, then it's all okay, everything will be okay, we'll work it out."

Dr Tim Sharp of Australia's 'Happiness Institute' says, "Humour is a core component in resiliency, and one reason for that is because it's about seeing things from a different perspective; something that all the best cartoonists and comedians do. The happiest and most successful people don't just stop at one way of looking at a situation; they'll explore other ways."

Rick Wilson backs this up from his own experience, "People who can't find humour in anything who don't have that sense of joy, even the shitty moments, they are much less able to handle these things."

We can't really talk about resilience without referring to Viktor Frankl, who has said that a sense of humour is the key characteristic to resilient survival of traumatic events. In his writing on survival in concentration camps under the Nazi regime, he says, "Humor was another of the soul's weapons in the fight for self-preservation. It is well-known that humor, more than anything else in the human makeup, can afford an aloofness and an ability to rise above any situation, even if only for a few seconds."

This ability is so commonplace that we even have a language for it, including 'dark humour', 'gallows humour' and 'black comedy'. Various TV shows and movies using this theme encourage us to laugh at events which we might otherwise feel outraged, disgusted, offended or even scared by.

There seems to be an endless source of academic research into the relationship between humour and resilience. It's perhaps not surprising - if the human race could learn how to better face adversity and overcome our shared challenges, we might enjoy longer life, improved relationships and reduce the cost of healthcare.

Al Siebert, founder of the 'Resiliency Center', discovered in 2010 that "Laughter and playfulness are key skills for the survivor personality." He found that the ability to use playful humour and laughter in adversity is powerful, providing a new perspective, redefining the emotional meaning of the situation and leads to more effective actions. He says, "Playing with a situation makes a person more powerful than sheer determination. The person who toys with the situation creates an inner feeling of 'This is my plaything; I am bigger than it... I won't let it scare me. I'm going to have fun with this."

Rutter[22] (1985) found that resilient individuals have a sense of humour when facing challenging circumstances. Tugade and Frederickson[23] (2004) discovered that resilient people are those who use positive emotions in their recovery from negative experiences.

Wolin and Wolin[24] (1993) investigated the connection between creativity and humour in resilient people. In using humour in creative ways, the person moves past being a victim when they find ways to laugh about their situation. One of the essential skills for surviving and rising above adversity is the ability to turn "nothing into something, and something into nothing" by using creativity and humour.

Researchers at Harvard University have been tracking the health of a group of students since 1938. Psychiatrist George Vaillant, who joined the team as a researcher in 1966, led the study from 1972 until 2004. He says, "When the study began, nobody cared about empathy or attachment. But the key to healthy ageing is relationships, relationships, relationships."

In the book *Aging Well*, Vaillant wrote that six factors predicted healthy ageing for the Harvard men: physical activity, absence of alcohol abuse and smoking, having mature mechanisms to cope with life's ups and downs, and enjoying both a healthy weight and a stable marriage. For the inner-city men, education was an additional factor. "The more education the inner city men obtained," wrote Vaillant, "the more likely they were to stop smoking, eat sensibly, and use alcohol in moderation."

Of the many "mature mechanisms to cope with life's ups and downs" that are available to us, humour is one of the most important, both individually, and for preserving the integrity of the relationships which Vaillant finds to be so important.

There are many people in our society who do very tough, demanding, challenging jobs that I am certainly grateful for. Often, those jobs can cause mental health problems through stress and the exposure to traumatic situations, and a sense of humour is vital, both in coping with the job and also with avoiding other coping mechanisms which might be less healthy.

Comedian and writer Kevin Day spent some time working in the ambulance service and saw first hand how this works. "Every job has its own different type of humour. One of my closest friends is still a paramedic and you learn from working in the ambulance service, and being amongst ambulance crews and firemen, that they have the blackest, bleakest sense of humour, but they have to, because they're not going to get through the day unless they can distance themselves from what they've seen and what they've done. They're never going to sleep at night without the aid of alcohol. So they find a way and their mechanism is humour, because they have to dehumanise the people they've dealt with. That sounds horrible but it's partly why they're so good at their job. If they start to get wrapped up with the people there, if they start to think, I wonder what happened to that old lady that I took in this afternoon, they won't be able to function. So they use humour amongst themselves, only amongst themselves."

You can see that in Kevin's example, the humour not only provides an individual coping mechanism, it also serves to create social bonding, a camaraderie that enables the members of a team to lean on each other through the darkest times.

Comedian turned crime writer Mark Billingham likens the contrast found in humour to crime fiction. "In order for the dark to be truly dark, there has to be light so you can compare the two. I learned that hitting very hard and keeping it going and keeping the pages turning you have to keep the laughs coming. Crime fiction is all about timing. It is all about the reveal. It is all about that moment, similar to a joke, where the audience thinks the punch line is coming from one direction, then it hits them from somewhere else."

Life will inevitably throw you a series of curve balls. Your attitude won't stop nasty surprises, but it will help you to bounce back quicker, and perhaps even stronger.

To say that Ebony Rainford-Brent is a cricketer is an understatement. Wikipedia describes her thus; "Ebony-Jewel Cora-Lee Camellia Rosamond Rainford-Brent FRSA is an English cricket commentator and former cricketer, who was the first black woman to play for the England team. During her playing career, she was also captain of the Surrey women's team. Rainford-Brent was a member of the England team that won the 9th ICC Women's Cricket World Cup held in Australia from 9–22 March 2009. England beat New Zealand by 4 wickets in the final held at North Sydney Oval on 22 March 2009. In the three months following their World Cup win, the team went on to win the final of the 2009 ICC Women's World Twenty20, the NatWest One Day series 4–0 against Australia, and also retain the Women's Ashes."

If you don't understand the technical cricket jargon, this means that the team that she played in did very, very well. Perhaps better than anyone had expected. Certainly better than their performance up to that point would have predicted. I'll let Ebony explain what changed.

"I've been in the team that won the World Cup back in 2009. I was with the team for 18 months in the build up to that. When I started, we were losing everything. I remember us going out to the World Series in Chennai, and it was four teams and we pretty much finished but lost every match. There was no lightness in the atmosphere, we struggled to connect, struggled sometimes to have difficult conversations, just all of those things were part of it. There was a point, like a line drawn in the sand, by captain Charlotte Edwards, where we decided to start singing a song by Take That, called *Never forget*. The song was sung every time we won a game, just remember where we came from. But once we started singing the song after each game, we won, we didn't take the mick out of each other how we sang, how bad or good we played, it just started bringing the team together. We used it as an anchor every time we won for 18 months, and we ended up going on this incredible win run and winning two World Cups, so there's no doubt that bringing all of that jovial aspect, lightening the changing room, maybe making it easier to sometimes tackle difficult conversations is really important."

Penny Mallory turned her early start in life to an asset, yet still needed a healthy dose of humour to pull everything together. "Well, you of course you have to be resilient, and that's about relentlessness. It's about being so fixed on that one thing that nothing will stand in your way, which means you've got to be prepared to knock every obstacle, you'll find a way around it, through it, under it, over it, whatever, because nothing will stand in your way. in order to have that sort of discipline and relentlessness, you have to lighten that load with some humour. It's that ability to laugh and let off some steam because it's really intense. It's really heavy. It has a potential to drag you down if you can't balance it with some laughs and some funny stuff."

Cally Beaton reflects on the experience of failure in the world of comedy, and the importance of making sure you still leave other people feeling good, because they don't necessarily know that anything is going wrong from your point of view. "Most comedians are very insecure, if there's one thing that didn't go well, that's the thing we'll remember so we'll come offstage and ask, 'Oh, why did I mess up that joke?' 'Why did I forget that bit?' 'Why did I trample over my own applause break?' Occasionally you will see people who are the other extreme, someone will have an abysmal gig but then come off with massive swagger, not just I'm going to style this out, but genuinely, they think they had a good gig. If I had a gig like that and thought that was a good gig, I would be ignoring the feedback from the room. Most comedians believe that it's never the audience, it's always us. So you can't come off and go, 'Oh, well, it was a Saturday night and they were really drunk, or the lighting wasn't great, or the tech guy messed up my microphone', at the end of the day it's on you. It's for you to save, make or break the time you're on stage. How would you fail better if you didn't even know you failed? So I'm very aware when I fail, which is frequently and flamboyantly.

If something's going to go wrong, it's more likely to happen in a comedy club than in a corporate. I hosted one award show where everything that could possibly have gone wrong went wrong, including the fact that the lapel mic didn't work, the headset mic didn't work, and then the radio, and then the handheld battery ran out. I ended up doing about an hour and a half on stage with no mic. I thought that if I leave then no-one is going to have any sympathy for the fact that that I was left in impossible situation. Everyone in the room will think 'that was a real Prima Donna and you ruined our night'. I had to make the decision, I have decided to stay, I am in charge of these people's evening, they've all put their hat in the ring for an award, they're really excited to know if they're going to get one. They don't care if the host has had all these problems. So I have to somehow be gracious and fun and nice to them because it's completely not their fault. You have to have that attitude of humility, of 'I'm here to make you all feel good'."

Humourology

How to keep your chin up

"Humour is a great tonic for your mental health."

Dave Johns

At times, when things look rough, it can be hard to think of any other way to see the situation, let alone think of funny things to say about it. As Monty Python told us,

"Some things in life are bad

They can really make you mad

Other things just make you swear and curse

When you're chewing on life's gristle

Don't grumble, give a whistle

And this'll help things turn out for the best

And.. Always look on the bright side of life…"

Michael Fenton Stevens recalls the moment that all-round entertainer and TV presenter Roy Castle was given a terminal diagnosis, surely the worst news that anyone can hear. "I remember lovely Roy Castle who said that when he went to the doctors, they said to him 'I'm really sorry, but you've got lung cancer. You've got six months to live.' Roy Castle said 'I can do it in three.'

Here's my advice for how to use humour when things are taking a turn for the worst.

Step back

We know that it's important to get a wider perspective on the situation, but that can be the most difficult to do, so if you can't step back mentally or emotionally, then step back physically. It can be that simple, just step right back, away from what's going on, and you'll see a broader set of events and relationships playing out. If you can't physically step back because the situation isn't right there in front of you then that's a hint that you're carrying the situation around in your head, and you then have to step back from yourself to get a new perspective. One way to do that is to look in a mirror and see yourself in your environment. Another way is to change your shoes.

Change your shoes

The comedian Steve Martin said, "Before you criticize a man, walk a mile in his shoes. That way, when you do criticize him, you'll be a mile away and have his shoes."

One of the most important things that can happen when you step into someone else's shoes is that you can see yourself in a different way. Brand and culture expert Jon O'Donnell says, "Humour is often a manifestation of vulnerability. You're showing someone that you are able to have a laugh at your own expense. The handshake was supposedly developed to demonstrate that you weren't concealing a weapon, and so it allowed people to feel more comfortable. Humour is a similar thing. If you meet somebody and you make them feel at ease and you make them smile, you make them laugh, it makes them immediately think, this person isn't a threat."

International speaker Marisa Peer agrees: "You must be able to laugh at yourself, that's really important."

Comedian Marcus Brigstocke relates perspective to humility, which is a very important trait when we're trying to build personal connections. "If you're incapable of finding yourself funny, or the things you do, amusing, or acknowledging that you are capable of being laughable, then a piece of your humanity is missing. You have no humility. If you can't laugh at yourself, you've got no humility. You might, for a moment, be a good leader. You might be exactly who's needed to achieve a certain task but as a fully functioning human being, if you're incapable of finding others funny, and of finding yourself funny then there's a piece of you missing."

A friend of mine developed an unpleasant reaction to garlic for which his doctor prescribed a short course of ointment and suppositories. He took the prescription to the pharmacy, presented it at the counter and waited patiently for the pharmacist to make the necessary arrangements. After a few minutes, the pharmacist, standing at the far back of the shop, shouted at the top of her voice, "I've got your ointment but I'll have to order in your suppositories!"

Following a short yet intensely uncomfortable silence, she came forwards to the counter and said, "Sorry, I shouted that, didn't I?"

"Yes. Yes, you did.", was my friend's quiet reply.

I asked him how he was able to see the funny side of such an embarrassing incident and he said, "If I was standing in the shop and this had happened to someone else, it would have been hilarious. So it's no less funny, just because it happened to me."

The acid test that my friend uses in such situations is simple: Would it be funny if it happened to someone else? If yes, then it's funny.

Imagine yourself standing in someone else's place, seeing what they can see, hearing what they can hear. Notice how things look different from their angle. Henry Ford said, "If there is any one secret of success, it lies in the ability to get the other person's point of view and see things from that person's angle as well as from your own." It turns out that this isn't just the secret of success, it's also the secret of getting a new perspective and increasing your resilience. Once you are standing in someone else's shoes, you may find it easier to 'see the funny side' with the bonus, as Steve Martin said, that you'll have someone else's shoes.

Lean on me

Learn to get by with a little help from your friends. Having someone to talk to about setbacks and problems is hugely important, but do make sure you're not talking to the same person and trying to drag them into your problems. It actually helps to talk to someone who you don't automatically agree with, who can help you to find that different perspective that's so important. Be there for your friends to lean on, too. One of the obstacles in building your resilience is not being able to get out of your own head, and a friend can help you to do that by pointing out other ways to interpret the situation.

Make time for yourself

When your life revolves around the situation that's causing the problem, it's hard to get any distance from it. On the other hand, if you can't wait to rush home from work to attend to your children, pets or stamp collection, or you look forward to the weekend when you can go fishing or play sport, then your life has a broader context which puts the problematic situation into a more natural perspective.

Comedian and actor Dave Johns sums it up perfectly; "Having humour is a way of getting through bad times, if you can laugh at stuff and laugh at yourself. You don't take yourself too seriously. That's a great tonic for your mental health."

Humourology

Ebony Rainford-Brent says, "It's okay to fail and when things get tense, when there's no space to fail or to get something slightly wrong, you feel under pressure to just deliver without any sort of flexibility, when there's a little bit of humour that you could have with a chief executive or with a member of staff or whatever it is that there's a little bit of flexibility is okay, and we don't have to take this over intensely, as long as we're learning and we're growing. That's the underlying message. the other side is using humour to celebrate success. It's okay then when you do actually learn from your failures, and you come back, you can come back and celebrate and wind people up, you didn't think we got it, that sort of stuff. It's so important to be able to fail, it's so important to be in an environment where you don't want to ever make anyone feel uncomfortable, but you can have just a little bit of give and take with each other as well just allows that environment to be able to fail better, and then keep growing and learning very quickly.

Georgie Holt, Managing Director of Acast recognises that it's sometimes difficult to find the funny side of a situation, and in such instances, perhaps a funny friend can lend a hand. "Sometimes there isn't humour in everything. I absolutely know that. But if you can find it, if you can cling on to it, and you can keep it close to you, you'll be surprised how quickly scenarios and situations become diffused either internally or externally. I'd also advise anyone to find someone who makes you laugh as well. I quite often, in tough or intense situations in work or in life, try and find someone who makes me laugh quite quickly afterwards because I just want to have that emotion and physical release of laughter. I would always know the two or three people I would try to find after a tough negotiation or client conversation, who would level the situation and make me laugh at myself, the situation or something else entirely. I found that an amazing, amazing tool to process feelings. I always felt it was easier after the fact, after the laughter."

Jimmy Mulville reminds us that a problem shared is better than keeping it all inside. "What is the point of comedy? Well, it makes people laugh. It's involuntary. It's very good for the circulation. It makes you feel joined up to other people and also it fulfils a very serious role of reducing very difficult and frightening concepts to a size that we can all enjoy."

One of the easiest ways to put some distance between yourself and a problem is to wait. Time, as they say, is a great healer. John Lloyd had such an experience as a result of a TV show that he took part in. "I was a guest on *I've Never Seen Star Wars*. You undertake to do five things you've never done. I agreed to watch *The Wire*, read *The Curious Incident of the Dog in the Night Time*, milk a goat, do five minutes of stand up comedy, and the last thing was go back to school. I had built up this idea that I hated school. It was 40 years to the year that I went back. I realised I didn't hate it at all. I hated some of it but a lot of it was great, and entertaining and fun nights, great friends. It was like a weight being lifted. You see your formative years as being awful but that wasn't true. It really let lightness into my heart, after 40 years of being resentful about it. This is extraordinary. The stories we tell ourselves about who we are that aren't actually true."

The stories we tell ourselves; a recurring theme from many of my guests. You can tell yourself that you failed, or you can tell yourself that you learned, and had fun along the way. It's your choice.

Failure is definitely an option

"Unless you risk failure, you learn nothing."

Scott Quinnell

Never be scared to fail. Failure is essential. Failure is the most important part of the process. Unless you are willing to put yourself in a position to fail, you will never grow. You will never accomplish anything worth doing because those people who succeed are often on a razor's edge between success and failure. They are bold. They are unlike other people.

You do not learn much from success. In all the years that I performed on stage at London's Comedy Store, I never learned anything on the nights that the audience watched politely and quietly. I only learned on the nights that they laughed, heckled and, occasionally, threw bottles.

Only in failure do you really look closely at how you could improve. Only in that close examination are you able to learn what you really need to learn. Learning to laugh at your own failures simply moves you faster to a place where you can learn.

Comedian Adrian Walsh agrees. "Failure is not the opposite of success. It's part of it. As a young comic, it's only through failure you learn by doing things wrong, then you become better at it. Nobody, nobody starts good at anything."

Spike Edney is a musician who has performed with such household names as Queen, Ben E. King, Edwin Starr, Duran Duran, The Boomtown Rats, Dexys Midnight Runners, Bucks Fizz, Haircut One Hundred and The Rolling Stones. You can imagine the pressure to perform note-perfect, every night on a tour. "If you slip or come off the rails, you can either be sorry and apologise and then become negative or you can say 'What a cock-up, we can do that better' and turn it into a positive thing when it becomes a great moment in a show. That's the moment people will remember and take away." Conversely, the legendary Van Morrison is known for being an absolute perfectionist. "I remember there was no humour the afternoon I spent in Van Morrison's company. His band on their own were very funny, but the moment he walked in the room, they weren't funny any more. A humour handbrake situation."

Without learning there can be no perfection, and without humour, learning becomes more difficult.

One of the questions that people ask me most often is, "What gave you the strength to keep on going in your career? How did you manage to never give up?"

It's a good question, because when I first began, I had no idea how to keep going either. An important part of it was the people I surrounded myself with.

When I wanted to make sure I couldn't back out of running my first marathon, I told forty people close to me in the six months beforehand in order to make sure that I saw it through. It's easy when you're making plans for your life to keep them to yourself, just in case you change your mind.

Creating your own deadlines is an excellent way to keep on track but what's more important is that you share those commitments with others. That's not to lay the responsibility or blame on other people, it's to have other people ask you, "How's it going? How's the preparation? Are you nervous?" and so on. It's about connecting your goal with a bigger importance, it's not just about you because nothing ever is. Everything we do is for others, and depends on others. We're part of a network. When you add the power of humour to your network, you can achieve even greater things.

How can you do that? Simply by carefully choosing the people you tell about your dreams and big plans. Choose friends, colleagues and relatives who will joke with you, poke fun at you, lift your spirits and also give you a different perspective when the going gets tough.

It's easy to surround yourself by people who have high expectations of you, or who are 'into' whatever you're embarking on and take the subject very seriously. This can be dangerous because it can make you feel defensive about failure. You don't want to admit when things aren't going to plan because you don't want to disappoint the people who have high expectations or be ridiculed by the people who think that they can do it better than you.

It's your fear of failure, of letting people down, of being rejected, of not being good enough, of not living up to the expectations of others that will cause you to fail.

What's important is how you use that fear. This is very much on Scott Quinnell's mind when he's on the Rugby pitch.

"The fear, to me, is transferred into adrenaline. Adrenaline is transferred into positive energy. Positive energy turns into outcome. As long as you can channel that, and you can express the fear, and you can go into it and face it, there's no better feeling at the start of the game.

That's the only part I miss of rugby. I don't miss the playing any more. I don't miss the training any more. I do my own type of training. I miss that buzz in the changing room before the game. I've said it before, when you get those butterflies, the closer you get to the game, the bigger, the stronger they get. If they're not there, then there's something wrong. I'm not getting that feeling on the Rugby pitch any more, I'm getting it when I stand up in front of 2000 people and talk about my story.

If you don't feel that fear, that energy, then it's time to give up. It's the positivity of turning that fear into something wonderful. The fact that when those butterflies, when those nerves come, that's when you get the best of yourself because complacency doesn't set in. There's nothing better than standing on the edge of that cliff the first time that you're going to do something new, to push yourself.

Sometimes the fear can be not wanting to fail, and when you go out there, and things don't work, or the game doesn't go well, or the speech, you go out there, and it doesn't quite work. It's adapting and knowing that you can go and do it again, but maybe do it slightly differently.

That's why comedians go on warm-up tours for six months to get enough material to do a two-hour show. People see the two hour show; they don't see the six months in the build up. Failure means success in the end because you learn, you hone things. Unless you risk failure, you learn nothing and you have no new material, or fresh ideas, or whatever it is for you.

Sometimes I stand there when things don't quite go well, or I'm on live television and I say something I shouldn't say. Afterwards, I just think, 'Ha-ha, I can't believe I just said that. It's brilliant!' Don't be frightened to say something because if you never say anything, you never make any mistakes. The only way to never make a

Humourology

mistake, to never fail, is to do nothing, to stay home, stay safe. You have to ask yourself which is more important for you."

Jimmy Mulville also recognises the power of humour to vanquish fear. "What is the point of comedy? It makes people laugh. It's involuntary. It's very good for the circulation. It makes you feel very joined up to other people. It fulfils a very serious role of reducing difficult and frightening concepts to a size that we can all enjoy."

When I work with clients to help them develop their presenting and pitching skills I tell them to "Look forward to things going wrong because that is when you have the most fun." The psychological effect of 'looking forward to things going wrong' reframes the idea of failure, because it's only when things don't turn out how we expected that we really discover what we're made of.

Self-help guru John La Valle takes the same approach when he's coaching executives. "Look forward to stuff going wrong because that's when you're going to have the fun. That's when it's going to humanise you, that's going to make people say, he's a real person, I've connected with her."

I performed regularly at London's Comedy Store through the 1990s when improvisational comedy was in its heyday. The audience was mostly made up of visitors to London, tourists attracted by the Comedy Store's location and reputation. We could have done the same show every night, who would have known? That's the rut that a lot of performers get into, they forget that there's an audience there. It doesn't matter whether it's a new audience or the same one, when the performer just goes through the motions, the performance loses its edge. A new audience can see that just as much as someone who has seen the show a dozen times before. You might think that a performer can't really plan for that, and especially for the improvisational work that we were doing, because how can anyone rehearse when they don't know what suggestions the audience will come up with? Well, as a minimum, we knew what time we'd start and finish. We knew the audience would be asked to make suggestions, characters, relationships, places, that kind of thing. We knew that we would improvise scenes around those suggestions. So we could rehearse, both physically and mentally, for those constants, the things we knew would happen. Then, on the night itself, we didn't have to stop and think what we were doing next, we could be in the moment, involving the audience, playing on their laughs, enjoying the spontaneity, and every show was exactly the same as every other, and at the same time, totally different and unique.

At the very least, when something goes wrong, you'll have a funny story to tell about it, which is exactly what happened to Bobby Kerr. "There's a period of reflection between the failure and the moving on, which could be as little as an hour, or it could be a week, or it could be a month, but there should be some period, depending on how big the screw up actually is. When I worked in Canada, in the mid 1980s, I was involved in the Pope's visit to Canada. It was a big airport, an old military base, about 30 miles north of Toronto, and the company I was working for, we're doing all the catering, huge logistical operations, with massive big trailers and trucks and living in camper vans. I was on the site and my job was to run this and they were expecting a million people, that was the forecasted visitors on the day. The event was in September, so in July or June of that year, we froze 500,000 sandwiches under liquid nitrogen. Three days

Humourology

before the Pope arrives, it rains, cats and dogs. Torrential rain, the site becomes a mud bath. It was like a scene out of Father Ted, priests and nuns rolling around in the mud. The day happens and of the million that were expected to come, 100,000 people came and 50% of them brought their own sandwiches. The company that I was working for lost over a million dollars on the day. My boss was fired. I remember thinking, this is failure. Fail fast, fail big."

Be certain that what you are doing is worth persevering with. You need to make sure that you can still remember why you're doing it, and that you're still doing it for the right reasons. Just take a moment to think back to the decision that you made to embark on this project or journey. Be honest with yourself, were you doing it for yourself or for someone else? What did you hope to gain from it?

Every goal has to have some personal gain in it. No matter what that gain might be, it's certainly easier to keep going when you know exactly how you will benefit. Perhaps the best personal benefits include self respect and the knowledge that you succeeded in spite of any setbacks, because ultimately, when you find the strength and courage to keep going, what you overcome is not any external obstacle. What you have overcome is your own doubt.

When you think back to why you're on this path, you might also think about other times in the past when you have proven yourself to be right, so that you can remind yourself of what worked for you.

Remember, too, that when you give up once, you make it far more likely that you will give up again next time. When you begin to rationalise or play down your surrender, you make it acceptable, and that is most certainly not acceptable. If you decide that it is better to stop and turn back, you will ideally feel bitter disappointment, because you have made a decision based on insurmountable external obstacles. If you have to rationalise the decision to turn back, you're soothing your conscience and trying to make yourself feel better. Your doubts have won, and you must never allow this to happen.

By reminding yourself why you started on this particular journey, you recommit to it. It's important to keep communicating this to the team too, reminding them of what it is that first inspired them.

All too often, people get so bogged down in the details and minor setbacks that they lose sight of the overall objective that was the original source of their enthusiasm. Since your team are probably going to be much closer to those details and setbacks than you are, it is vital that you keep that inspiration firmly in their minds.

I'm not saying that you should be blindly confident or plough on regardless, thinking that if you ignore the obstacles, they'll go away. The reality is that you have much work yet to do. What you're doing is reminding yourself and your team of why it's all worthwhile.

An important part of making a commitment to your goal is to burn your bridges. If you set out on a difficult project or journey with a plan B in the back of your mind, you are giving yourself an excuse, a way out, before you have even started. You make it easier to go back. This is not the same as a lifeline, because a lifeline gives you a way to return to a safer position so that you can try again. A lifeline is a way to make it safer to achieve your goal, whereas a plan B is a way to give up on your goal.

Make public commitments, get sponsorship, even write yourself a mission statement and pin it to your wall. Make sure that, when you succeed, it's for you and when you give up, you have everyone else to answer to, including your team. These public commitments are a sign for them too.

In building such a high level of commitment to the vision and goals of the team, it is important not to lose sight of the steps that lie immediately in front of you.

Break the overall objective down into realistic steps. Don't think in terms of breaking the objective down into easy steps though. How many houses have you been to where the owners tried to make their renovation project easy to achieve by doing a bit at a time? They end up in a bigger mess than they started with. When you break down the objective, make your steps logical and thorough. Plan short term goals that keep you moving and keep you focused on what you can achieve, right now. When you plan those short term goals properly, you can occasionally step back and see how much closer you are to your end objective.

Other people are full of good advice. Some people tell you what you want to hear, some offer enthusiastic encouragement and some can come up with endless reasons why your project is doomed to failure. Ultimately, most people will tell you what they would do if they were in your shoes. They are not in your shoes. Again, remember the wise words of comedian Steve Martin, "Before you criticize a man, walk a mile in his shoes. That way, when you do criticize him, you'll be a mile away and have his shoes."

If you solicit advice, be careful that you aren't only asking for the advice that you want to hear. If you're thinking of giving up, you might only listen to the negative advice. That might convince you that it's better to give up, or it might make you want to prove them wrong. Ultimately, in your heart, you know exactly what you need to hear in order to get the motivation that you want. Remember the old saying, a camel is a horse designed by a committee. Never give up your control and your choice. This is your journey, your goal, and you must think for yourself.

When you have negative thoughts, which are natural and normal, it's good to catch them and acknowledge them. You don't have to sit down and have a heart to heart about them, you might diffuse them with some humour and this is where it really helps to have a friend who will lift your spirits by making fun of you, or finding some humour within the events. The important thing is that when you have a negative thought, keeping it to yourself amplifies it and before long it becomes your new focus, your new goal. When you have a negative or destructive thought, say it, express it, exorcise it. Be very careful not to do this in front of your team, though. They may not always be able to tell the difference between shaking off negative thoughts and the warning signs of you giving up.

It helps to step back and get a broader perspective of your failure. When you think about some of the things you have achieved in the past, you can see that your current situation is easily within your capabilities. You can see not only where you need to be but also how far you have come.

Of course, you still need to be realistic. When you step back and look at the reality of your situation, you can also see a realistic way forward for you. Planning for setbacks doesn't make you pessimistic, it makes you realistic.

Humourology

If planning for setbacks makes you feel that it's not even worth trying, you're being pessimistic. If planning for setbacks makes you find alternatives and gives you more determination, you're being realistic.

However you see the bigger picture, the system that you are a part of and the network of people who rely on you, you can understand that you are where you are right now because of the choices that you made, and that means that you are in control of your situation and your destiny.

I've heard so many leaders paraphrase the NASA quote and say to their teams 'failure is not an option'. Not only is it a terrible cliché, it's not even true – failure must be an option if you are to learn and grow. In fact, if innovation, growth and learning are your goals then failure is your only option if you want to learn how to get up to fight another day.

All the world's a stage

Laughter is a feeling of acceptance

Jon Plowman

William Shakespeare's works are well known for the use of comedy in the midst of tragedy. In fact, all of his tragedies include a clown.

You'll no doubt be familiar with the symbol of the theatre - the masks of comedy and tragedy which symbolise the contradictory nature of the human condition.

The most obvious Shakespearean example is the Fool in *King Lear* who makes jokes out of the King's predicament and is permitted, under the guise of foolery, to criticise him. Shakespeare's tragedies include a minor character who makes jests at the expense of the tragic actors and often takes the position of the audience in seeing the ridiculous nature of the predicament. Shakespeare was not the first writer to do this, Christopher Marlowe's tragedy *Doctor Faustus* features a clown parodying the ambition of the play's main character, leading him to sell his soul. Hamlet has the grave-digger joking about mortality. The Porter in *Macbeth* joked about the effect of alcohol on a man's sexual performance, something which sat at the very heart of the play's darkness. Even *Othello* has a Clown. In Act 3, Scene 1, a scene rarely included in modern productions, *Othello*'s Clown mocks Cassio with jokes about sexually transmitted diseases which Cassio seems not to understand, enacting the naivety about sexual motives that lies behind the tragedy.

Many modern films are based on Shakespeare's stories and equally balance comedy and tragedy. Many comedians go on to become excellent actors, perhaps because of their hard-earned mastery of timing and audience engagement.

Robin Williams' performance in *The Fisher King* begins as a portrait of a crazy homeless guy and quickly reveals the dark side of his terrible, heart-wrenching secret. The plot features the redemption of Jeff Bridges' character as he helps Williams to come to terms with these two opposing sides of his personality and in doing so, acknowledges his own part in the tragic story.

The British cult classic *Withnail and I* is crammed with dark humour as 'I' narrates the story of two struggling actors who lurch drunkenly from one unsettling predicament to the next. The real tragedy is the sense of loss at the end of the film, that one character can evolve and the other cannot, being forever trapped in the past.

Yasmin Alibhai-Brown notes that the balance of tragedy and comedy isn't unique to Western stories. "Shakespeare saw that in the most tragic of plays, he'll bring in the clowns as if to make it bearable, the light and shade. You have to have the clowns even in the deepest tragedy. In Indian movies, it was the same. Whatever was going on, there were these comic characters that would be injected sometimes willy-nilly into the plot to lift the spirits of the audience and those were quite unforgettable movies. There is a need to release. It's almost like a valve."

You can observe this fine balance of laughter in pain in so many comedians-turned-actors that I can't even begin to name them all. Jim Carrey, Lesley Nielsen, Lee Evans, Bill Murray, Steve Carrell, Steve Coogan, Gene Wilder, Richard Pryor, Steve Martin, Lily Tomlin, Woody Allen, Bette Midler, Whoopi Goldberg… I could go on and I'm sure that you can think of more.

The theatrical masks perhaps remind us that comedy and tragedy are interwoven, that one can lead to the other and that you have the power to redefine any tragedy in life as a comedy of errors and to reassure yourself in the knowledge that all's well that ends well.

Kindness

"Humour allows you to hold on to hope."

Tessy Ojo

As Steve Martin's character said in the film *Planes, Trains and Automobiles*, "Kindness? KINDNESS?"

Yes, kindness. It could seem to be such an ethereal, vague, unimportant concept. Maybe it simply means that you treat people how you would like to be treated. The problem is that you often don't treat yourself very kindly. You put yourself down and put yourself last. You pre-empt criticism by criticising yourself. Through all of that, you miss out on opportunities for praise, recognition and even love because you afraid of hearing the opposite. So if you are to be kind to others, you have to bite the bullet and start with yourself.

Is there a link between humour and kindness? Children's author Giles Paley-Phillips thinks so.

"Comedy is a way of poking fun at things. As a species, we should learn to be able to take jokes ourselves, to take little pokes and prods ourselves in the way we do things.

On a medium like Twitter, for example, it's very difficult, things like politics or football have become intertwined as tribalism. There's a lack of nuance now, particularly on social media where people take things to heart a little bit more, but it's so important for us all to have a sense of humour. That's got to be our first thing, to not take ourselves too seriously in life.

Whatever you're going through, it is really important to dig into those feelings of kindness.

There's a philosophical question, whether there could be an act of kindness that isn't selfish in some way because when we are kind or we're nice or we're positive or we say something funny, we're getting something out of that as ourselves, but that's a good thing. Because if you're going through a difficult time, and when I'm feeling down or anxious, I lean into those sorts of things because they often make me feel better, they lift my mood. Obviously, if you're doing that for someone else, it's lifting their mood as well. So you're both having these moments where you're feeling lifted, or empowered, or inspired, whatever it might be. It's really important to lean into those things, those moments and try to utilise them for yourself as well as other people.

I feel very grateful to be here, I've had some very difficult moments along the way. I've had a lot of loss in my life, so I feel grateful for every day that I'm waking up and being in this world. Yes, not every day doesn't come without its challenges. But at the same time that level of gratitude allows me to push some of that stuff back out into the world and to model that for others. Being able to model kindness, compassion, empathy, a lot of us have forgotten to do this and maybe it's harder sometimes on social media because some people do want to use those platforms to vent and rage. But also those platforms are there to connect with one another.

It's social media, not anti social media. It's for connecting with people, having conversations, learning more about ourselves and the world through that connection. If I can, in some small way, create a community that is doing something more positive and light-hearted and kind then that's become a bit of a mission.

It is within us to make a positive change in life. Kindness and gratitude and happiness and positivity are within us and we have the power to remember those things, to empower those things in ourselves and to react in a certain way as well. We have to create those moments and actually think to ourselves, do I want to be happy today, do I want to be positive today? Do I want to put my energy into good things today? In any normal day there are little tests, but it's how you handle each of those tests and how you lead yourself through them. We can always do it in a positive way. There's always an option to be positive or kind or to take something with humour. There is always that within us."

In the end, people will remember you for how you make them feel, something that even Omid Djalili's mother knew when she said that people won't remember your jokes, they will only remember the joy that they felt. "They won't remember anything. They try to remember the jokes, they want to remember everything, but they'll just have a memory of being joyful.

Joy is an element in people's lives that is very much lacking. If you can give it to them, it's so precious, it's the main thing they'll remember. So humour was always used as a tool to implement joy. They never saw a human being funny as an end in itself, it was always a means to an end. So they said, we should use humour and jokes to get to the end of joy, because that's what they remember and that's what they'll talk about."

Joy is, of course, only one of an infinite variety of emotions that you can convey to others through the way you make them feel. If you knew that you had complete freedom over how you influence the feelings of others, why wouldn't you choose joy and laughter?

Tessy Ojo CBE is the Chief Executive of the Diana Award, a charity legacy to Diana, Princess of Wales' belief in the power that young people have to change the world, with the right support.

"When we were set up as a charity, it was really to instil the values that everyone so adored in Princess Diana, the values of empathy, kindness, selflessness, and just that ability to care deeply for other people without any gain. We are constantly helping instil those same values in young people because, as we've progressed as a society and as we've developed, we've also sadly lost some of the natural humaneness about our lives, that ability to connect with people, that ability to care, to be selfless. A lot of the time, we're in pursuit of self. It's got to be me, myself and I and that's such a dangerous place to be because that just gives us this tunnel vision where we care about nobody else except ourselves. We cannot build a society on selfishness, it has to be grounded in selflessness, compassion, empathy and understanding.

We all have the potential to sprinkle life with a bit of laughter and joy, just so that we live a better life."

Perhaps the most important aspect of resilience is knowing that, no matter how bad things have been, there is a brighter tomorrow waiting just around the corner. If we don't have hope then there's no point in having resilience.

Tessy Ojo sums it up perfectly. "The whole point of offering hope is to build resilience to say, 'we got this, we will make it, tomorrow will be a better day, better days are coming'. All those words are words that are completely geared towards me helping you build resilience for a later date, to give you assurance that the next day will be better, even if I don't know that for sure. What humour

Humourology

does is help you release those endorphins, helps you feel good, improves your mental well being and allows you to hold on to hope."

My late father Laszlo was born in Hungary. At 17 years old he was in the Second World War and was forced to fight with the Russian army, then held in a camp and was finally sent back to Hungary. When the Hungarian uprising happened, he had to escape again and was held in a refugee camp. This is a man who used to say, "I am lucky", because luck is an attitude. He could have complained about the hardships he had to endure, but instead he focused on his luck at surviving.

He would talk to strangers, befriend anyone, chat up my girlfriends when I was a young man and talk about his life as a triumph of hope over adversity. Above all else, he laughed. He laughed a lot. As Tessy Ojo said, "Humour allows you to hold on to hope."

⁴ Growing Your Funny Bone

"If you make someone laugh, it's a pleasure that doesn't cost any money so it's a life affirming thing that you can do that you don't need any equipment for."

Steve Coogan

I'm guessing that, by now, you're on board with the whole 'funny = money' concept. What you might now be wondering is, how does one actually learn to be funny? Or if you are one of the 100% of people in my research who said that they already have a good sense of humour, how do you learn to be funnier, or at least to tune your humour to the situation at hand?

Since Og the Hairy first took the open mic slot at The Cave and told the first joke using a woolly mammoth as a politically incorrect simile, comedians have used the same simple trick to refine their amusability and get funnier.

The trick is simple. Laughably simple, actually. If I just tell you what it is, you'll laugh and say, "That's ridiculous. There must be more to it than that."

Comedians are not like you. They are special people. This is the only possible explanation for the fact that when you tell a joke, a few people smile politely, but when that idiot on stage tells the very same joke, people roll in the aisles, holding their sides and wheezing to draw breath. The idiot on stage becomes all the more hysterical if he or she also appears with a crazy hairstyle and some kind of amusing apparel such as non-matching socks. If the posters advertising the 'gig' can also show them pulling a funny face, the night of your life is guaranteed.

I'm sure you've experienced something similar on a night out with colleagues or perhaps a dinner party with friends. You formulate an amusing quip, release it into the wild, no-one notices. Tumbleweed. Ten seconds later, your arch rival says the exact same thing that you said and everyone rejoices. I know, it's disheartening, but what it does reveal is that the joke, in itself, though brilliant, might not be the most important factor. What you might very well have discovered is the critical importance of

Humourology

timing.

Good timing will elevate the feeblest of puns and glorify the most inglorious of japes and whimsies. Bad timing will put down even the most side-splitting shaggy dog story. Why is timing so important?

Actor, comedian and presenter Sir Tony Robinson, best known for his role as a the downtrodden sidekick in the TV series *Blackadder* recalls a conversation about timing as a basic human instinct with the doctor, theatre director and presenter Dr. Jonathan Miller. "He spent the first third of his life living in humour. He moved away from it because there were things that interested him more, but I found it very interesting to talk to him about it. He said that humour is a fizz and it's like the bubbles of oxygen in your body. He thought that time was something to do with the rhythms in our body. Why would we all get timing the same? Why would we all fall about when somebody does a super bit of timing, unless it was something that was deeply shared within all of us?"

Timing is about anticipation and expectation. Remember, the essence of a good joke is conflict, and when the comedian supplies the punchline just at the right moment, not too soon and not too late, it satisfies the audience's need to resolve the conflict.

The comedian says, "What do you call a comedian who can't remember the punchline?"

The audience, inside their minds, screams, "For goodness sake, put us out of our misery, TELL US NOW!"

The audience anticipates that the conflict will be resolved, the answer will be supplied, and the audience and comedian will grow emotionally closer. So we know *why* timing is important in humour, but it doesn't answer the question of how to create the right timing, and it also doesn't answer the question of how to improve your humour, so let me address both of those by telling you the simple trick, which you will immediately reject for being too simple.

Before I get to that, I want to remind you of a very important fact, probably the most important fact of all. You are already funny. Neil Mullarkey agrees with me, "I believe that everybody can be funny. Everybody can make others laugh. All of us are funny with our friends. For me, humour is all about sharing our vulnerability. It's all about acknowledging we're all fragile and human."

Alistair McGowan agrees too, and likens it to the ability to sing. "My wife is a singer, a very, very good singer. She's done opera and musicals, everything. But she will still say everyone can sing. A lot of people who are in music will say everyone can sing and that's true if you catch people early enough. My voice teacher at Guildhall, Patsy Rodenburg is a brilliant, brilliant woman, and has written books about public speaking and everything to do with the voice. She would also say anybody can sing, but if someone gets into your head and says that you can't sing, you then get something which says I can't sing. Therefore, I don't listen. I don't believe I can sing and actually I can't because I'm not listening to the note because I've told myself I can't replicate it anyway. It's the same with humour. You know that anybody can be funny, but again, maybe they just aren't encouraged to be witty, or they just tell a joke once and it falls flat and they think they can't tell jokes.

When I started doing comedy, about 24, and went back to my home town at Christmas, I'd tell people what I was doing, and they would say, 'You? You're doing it?'

because I had given no hint of this. When I was young, I was not somebody who went around making people laugh at all, I was serious, I did sport, I did a bit of drama. I liked the comedy side of that, but I wasn't a witty person, I was very shy. That can stop people from being being funny. Listening is the most important thing. Are you listening to what's being said? Can you pick up on that so you can improve your funniness?"

You might be thinking that you've met people who were definitely not funny, and if humour is subjective then this might be true. Comedian, writer, actress and presenter Jo Brand believes that this is the case. "There are two types of humourless people; people who aren't funny and never try to be, and people who think they're funny, but they're not. The latter are worse because it's hard to break it to them that they're being annoying."

I prefer to think that everyone has the potential to be funny, and maybe it's just the wrong time and place, so here's a slightly different angle from comedian Marcus Brigstocke; "Everybody's funny to someone. It's just a question of finding that point of connection."

Everybody's funny to someone. Just pause and consider that idea for a moment. A good way to strengthen your funny bone is to start with the people who already share your sense of humour. Jo Brand goes on to temper her earlier comment, "Comedy is a very subjective thing so I accept that there are people who I think are funny, but someone else might not."

As Marcus Brigstocke said, "It's just a question of finding that point of connection."

I said that everyone is born with a sense of humour, and I've also said that your humour develops as part of your unique personality. You might think that some people are definitely funnier than others, and of course we could add 'to you' at the end of that statement. Growing your funny bone isn't necessarily about becoming more funny, this could also mean broadening the appeal of your humour.

Katrine Moholt makes time to practice humour, "You get stronger by using humour. The energy in the room when you're laughing and having a good time, that can heal you and it makes you stronger, it makes you feel good. It can help so much to work on it. We have to chase the happy moments, in the way that we're working on our daily exercise. We say to ourselves, today, I have to take the stairs, not the elevator and I don't need to eat that chocolate. Today, I must eat green or I have to have fruit today. In the same way, we think, 'Today, I am going to chase the happiness, the laughter'. By chasing the good times and chasing the humour, I'm working on laughing a little bit more than I did yesterday. I'm going to find the fun situations, I'm going to choose the fun situations. We can change ourselves to exercise it in the same way as exercising the physical body. As a parent you might think, 'Today, I want to make my children smile and laugh'. We want them secure and happy. We have to start with ourselves."

Graham Stuart is an award winning TV producer who has placed humour as a central theme of Graham Norton's successful TV talk shows. Having worked with countless celebrities, "people who are in the top echelon, the highest tier of what they are doing", Graham knows how to bring but humour. "You can absolutely improve and enhance your skills and be funny or be more interesting."

Adrian Walsh reflects on the process of testing and learning as an ongoing evolution. "Nobody, nobody starts good at anything. The biggest shock I got with today's young comics is that they're so much better than my generation were. They can go in and do five minutes and take chances, then go back and do another five minutes, then build that up. When I started off, I had to buy little joke books and we picked jokes out of that and put a little routine together. As you work with comics, they would give you bits, then you develop ideas, what makes you mad, what makes you happy, what makes you sad? What makes you angry, pick all those things, and then talk about it in a little microphone. Out of that will come the truth and you may only get two jokes, but if you do that every week, at the end of the week, you've got 14 jokes you may be able to use. You leave behind the old material and you you delve into your new stuff. You keep developing and from that, every generation brings with it its own ideas, its own culture, and develops it and makes it better than the last generation."

Often, people are funny without meaning to be. You might not laugh in their face but it becomes a funny story to tell afterwards. It's important not to make fun of the person but simply to recognise the weirdness of the situation. William Hague recalls such an instance in his work as a politician. "What always made me laugh as a Member of Parliament was encounters I had with my constituents that were just very genuine, people coming to my constituency surgery, not meaning to be funny. Somebody once walked in and I said, 'What can I do for you, madam?' and she said, 'Oh, I'm just looking.' I said 'What are you looking at? This is not a shop. This is my advice, my surgery.' She said, 'No, I thought I'd just come down here and have a good look at you for 10 minutes.' So she sat there having a good look, and then she went away. It keeps you down to earth if you have enough connection with people who do things like that, you can't take yourself too seriously."

I promised to share with you the simple secret to improving your humour, and here it is. The only difference between you and a professional comedian is that you censor your jokes before they have a chance to leave your mouth.

That's it. I told you that it was laughably simple.

You already have a 'style' of humour, and it's very easy to identify. Your 'style' is simply whatever makes you laugh. If it makes you laugh, it's tuned to your wavelength, and that's a good indication of what you can emulate to amplify your own humour signal. Your style of humour can also be found in the amusing comments which rattle around inside your head whenever you are able to look on the bright side or you notice something about life which makes you smile.

Bobby Kerr notes that what you find funny doesn't have to be shared by other people. "I often laugh at my own jokes, which is probably something you shouldn't do. My wife says I shouldn't. We've been married 33 years and worked together for nearly 40 years and she still doesn't think I'm funny.

Dr Richard Bandler also thinks it's important to begin by making yourself laugh. "I asked a judge once how he kept doing this year in and year out. He said, 'I may appear to be deadly serious, but on the inside, I'm telling myself jokes every minute.'"

Your humour doesn't have to be unique either. Think about stars such as Laurel and Hardy, the Marx Brothers, Harold Lloyd and Charlie Chaplin. They each had one joke, but they played that joke in a variety of situations.

Each use of their one joke created a unique connection with each unique audience, and that connection is so strong that you could be watching Laurel and Hardy in 1920 or 2020 and the joke would still work. The same basic formula of the 'odd couple' underpins almost every sitcom because it works, it is a recipe for conflict and therefore a recipe for resolving that conflict with humour. A simple formula, played out in infinite situations creates an infinite number of jokes, even though you could say that they are all variations on the same joke. Sitcoms have created odd couples that bridge the gaps that divide us as humans. Class, profession, gender, race, sexuality, political outlook and age are some obvious examples that I can think of. You can imagine the pitch to the TV studio...

"So it's an older conservative couple who live next door to a younger liberal couple?"

"That's right"

"Sounds hilarious! How much money do you want?"

You're unlikely to laugh continuously, all the way through a sitcom episode or Hollywood comedy, and there's an obvious reason for this - you're not expected to. Some jokes will resonate with you, some won't. Some will relate to your life experience, some won't. You identify with the characters who you feel a connection with, the ones whose style most closely matches your own.

The two aspects of timing and conflict could be summed up as 'surprise', as described by Jon Plowman. "Comedy is partly about surprise. When you meet somebody new you expect to shake their hand so if they then insult you, it's a nice surprise. Well, not always nice, but it's a good surprise and surprise, is at the heart of comedy. Changing the expectation is what good comedy does."

I've given you enough clues now, so let's put the puzzle together.

Both professional comedians and ordinary people with a reputation for being funny share the very same ability that you have. You have a sense of humour. You have the ability to find something amusing in life. You can see the funny side of things. As Dermot Murnaghan puts it, "Be yourself, whatever you are, and, and by and large, there is some humour in you somewhere." You can laugh a life's ups and downs. You are hard wired from birth to deal with conflict in your life, the dissonance between the world as it is and the world as you would like it to be, by seeing the funny side, by laughing in the face of misfortune. People who cannot do this might be described as humourless, arrogant, detached, emotionless - none of which are compliments. People who are unable to use humour in this way do find it harder to cope with life's ups and downs. One of the first things to suffer during times of depression is one's sense of humour. Laughter is a vital communication tool for social bonding. Laughter says 'we're in this together', and, 'we see things the same way'. A sense of humour is your birthright.

The professional takes this a stage further. Rather than censor their own jokes, they set them free and allow other people to judge. Inevitably, many of those jokes will fall flat, but enough will take flight and be rewarded with a laugh. The professional uses that positive feedback to tune their funny ideas. They will never have a 100% success rate, but what they will be continually doing is tuning to their immediate audience. With enough practice, they will learn to perform that tuning very quickly, giving the appearance that they are a social chameleon, able to fit in and make friends wherever they go. However, they're not 'good at telling jokes' or adept at creating puns or quips, they simply tell lots of jokes and learn from feedback. Any of their jokes that fall flat are simply forgotten and as a result, they are remembered only for being funny, or at least 'good humoured'. We are all naturally drawn to people who makes us feel good. Perhaps you've been to a wedding or other social event, and upon hearing laughter from another table as you gazed upon the stony countenances before you, thought, "I wish I was sitting over there instead."

Milton Jones connects humour as a way to create a shared truth, a way of laughing at something that brings people together in a shared experience. "Humour is loosely based on truth. We're all failed human beings, we all have things wrong with us and it's very healthy to know that you're not 'all it' and that we all make mistakes. Sometimes a speaker will get up and make a mistake, and not mention it and try and get away with it. If a comic does that he loses the trust of the crowd. It's very important to just have a realistic view of yourself and what you're doing so that people trust you. No company is perfect, no group of people have it all together, have learnt everything, because they will be far more successful if that were true. Humour fills in that gap between hope and reality. In its broadest definition, truth is a good thing. If you can make people resonate with what you're saying, That's a very healthy thing to do."

The reason that you censor your own jokes is that you think that if you don't get a laugh, you'll have offended someone or they will form an undesirable impression of you. When you do venture forth an amusing interjection only to be met with a stony silence, you feel embarrassed. You think that everyone is laughing at you, not with you. On the inside, of course. Externally, it appears that they didn't even hear you.

Don't be so full of yourself! What makes you think they're listening to you? What makes you think that they care about what you've said, at least enough to judge you for saying it?

When you don't make people laugh, they will not remember. When you make them laugh, they will remember, it's as simple as that. A comedian has to be spectacularly bad to be remembered for being bad. An average, mediocre comedian is forgotten - or rather, his or her jokes are forgotten. With persistence, they will be remembered. Tommy Cooper made an act out of being bad. His one joke was that he was so bad, either at performing magic tricks or at telling jokes, that he was very funny, and very popular. George Carl's one joke was to act as if he was clumsy whilst actually demonstrating breathtaking dexterity. Paul Zenon says, "The term clown is much maligned, but it's not just a curly wig or big shoes. It's someone like George Carl, who gets his finger stuck in his buttonhole, gets tangled up with a microphone lead or playing with his braces. It sounds like nothing, there's something very innocent about it, very irrational. I don't know why but it's funny."

The study of the structure of humour itself could fill several more books. People laugh in order to feel safe and in control. People laugh in order to minimise their embarrassment. People laugh in order to handle the stress of everyday life. You are at your funniest when you are being naturally funny, in other words, when you are saying something that makes *you* laugh. If it makes you laugh, it will also make people who are like you laugh.

I want to give you the simplest, easiest and most reliable route to strengthening your funny bone.

1. Start with what you find funny.

2. Get used to noticing your daily funny thoughts.

3. Set those funny thoughts and ideas free, by saying them out loud, writing them in your social media posts, even just writing them down on a notepad.

4. Notice which get the desired reaction and take a moment to reflect on why that was. Was it timing? Relevance? Anticipation? Something else?

5. Your funny thoughts and ideas will begin to change shape to strengthen your style.

Cally Beaton agrees with the first point, at least. "I met Joan Rivers and she said that I should take up stand up and two weeks later, I did my first gig. To quote the late, great Bob Monkhouse, 'Everybody laughed when I said I wanted to be a comedian. Well, they're not laughing now.' Now that always gets a laugh but I'm not pretending I came up with that. If you're a public speaker but you can't write jokes, just quote someone else's joke that's funny, or you could show a funny meme that made you laugh if you've got a lot of audio visual stuff. Start with what you find funny."

A friend of mine works in the field of corporate leadership development and, like most people these days, he regularly posts on social media. Disappointed at the engagement in his insightful posts on the nature of leadership, he tried an experiment. He posted a photo of a Rich Tea biscuit. That was all. It was one of his most popular posts ever. His lesson was that you have to be able to try something different and learn from feedback. Also, people like looking at biscuits.

Andy Hamilton is a comedian and writer whose work is behind many well known British sitcoms. This adds a new twist to the work of the Humourologist; creating humour through another person who is in turn creating an on-screen character. The writer has to create the mind of a character which is then embodied by the actor. The synergy between the writer and actor occasionally creates a character who lives on in our memories, long after the details of the story have been forgotten.

Andy says, "Sitcom acting is a really difficult craft because the actor is having to give a performance for 300 people sitting in front of them, but the performance has got to be the right size for the camera too. To make the story work, it's got to be natural, but they've also got to know where the laughs are, they've got to know where the beats are. It's highly technical and the ones who are really good managed to do all of that, to master the technical side, and also create a character who lives and breathes in people's homes. That is why audiences grow so affectionate towards those characters. The love that an audience will feel for a Del Boy or a Steptoe or even a nutcase like Basil Fawlty. The audience know that he's kind of mad but they still want to be in his company.

I write for the character and then once I cast the actor I can accommodate their speech and their rhythms. If you emphasise that word, it is funny and if you emphasise the other word, it is all knowing where to pause or knowing how brave to be with the pause. With some lines, there's probably more than one way of doing it and being funny so you experiment. A lot of great sitcom actors, in rehearsal, they're always ruffling the lines slightly, just trying out different permutations and then they decide which one they're most comfortable with."

What about timing, though? Thank you for reminding me. Remember *why* timing is important. You are answering the audience's question, at the exact moment they wanted you to answer it.

If you look at the behaviour of outstanding presenters, you'll see that they ask the audience a lot of questions. It actually doesn't matter whether those questions are intended to get a response or whether they are rhetorical questions, because the simple fact is that every question gets a response, doesn't it? Even if the presenter asks what seems like a rhetorical question, the audience will still answer, silently. That answer could be expressed as a nod or a smile, or even just the slightest tilt of the head or shift of posture. Whether the audience shout out their answers or keep them private, they do in fact answer, and so every question that the presenter asks creates an interaction. Every question forces the audience to engage. Too many questions and the audience starts to wonder if the presenter is going to share anything useful or concrete. Too few questions and the audience feels lectured at and their attention begins to wander.

If you want to develop your skills for presenting and public speaking, you might take a look at my books *The Pitching Bible* and *The Pocket Pitching Bible*.

How does an excellent presenter judge the right number or frequency of questions? Simply by observing what happens when a question is directed to the audience. If a question provokes a response, the frequency of questions is right. No questions will provoke a weaker response, and too many questions will lose the response.

Too few   **Just right**   **Too many**

Similarly, if a joke provokes a response, it was the right joke.

You might think that good comedians have an amazing ability to 'read' a room, to know what's appropriate and what isn't. It's true that even professionals comedians will get it completely wrong from time to time. Some have built a career out of teetering on the edge of offence, others have been just as successful by playing safe. When you're with your friends and family, you probably don't think twice about the comments you would share, as you have naturally developed a sense of being 'on the same wavelength'. At work, though, it's a different matter because you're not choosing the people you meet with, or at least, you're choosing to meet with them for reasons other than your shared love of 1950s sitcoms. You have something in common with the people you meet through work; perhaps a shared role, or a shared problem to solve. Whatever the link is between you, it's a link that you can strengthen with good humour.

Does that mean that you'll be making wisecracks and telling jokes all the way through a meeting to nominate people for the next round of redundancies? "Fred Bloggs in marketing? Well, he should be able to market himself eh? Eh? Amirite?"

Spike Edney recalls such an experience with someone who was funny, in small doses. "I once had the pleasure or misfortune to stand next to Frank Carson for an hour. That was the longest hour of my life because the first 15 minutes were glorious. In the last 45 I wanted to kill him because he just wouldn't shut up."

You might very well have a job that requires you to be serious, because the job you're doing is for people in trouble or distress, or simply for people who don't want to be made fun of. Remember what Kevin Day said about healthcare professionals, "So they use humour amongst themselves, only amongst themselves." Humour can be an important internal coping mechanism, it doesn't have to involve everyone. You're not performing for an audience, you're resolving your own conflict first.

One job in which humour definitely needs a light touch is that of an international diplomat. Diplomacy, in its very nature, requires being diplomatic, tactful, respectful of other customs and cultures. Yet, even in these circumstances, good humour can solve many problems when things go wrong, as they inevitably will. Remember what was written about Dr Henry Kissinger, "He made humor a tool of diplomacy ... Kissinger lightened the whole heavy international diplomatic scene."[25]

In his four years as Foreign Secretary, British politician William Hague had to learn how to apply all of his diplomatic skills to just such a complex, international stage where the world's media focuses on everything that you do.

"You have to be careful as foreign secretary, of course, because you're dealing with very serious situations, with the war and conflict and refugee flows and so on. So humour is less appropriate in the job of foreign secretary than in most jobs. Nevertheless, that there are amusing things that have happened. At the United Nations Security Council, I witnessed another Foreign Minister read out the speech of the wrong country. He just picked up his colleague's and he got well into this speech before he realised it couldn't possibly be his country that he was talking about. He was welcoming fellow Portuguese speakers to the council, and he wasn't a Portuguese speaker. It's not a rip roaring joke but things happen that you have to find amusement in when you're foreign secretary. Sometimes humour diffuses a situation in a private meeting and you can enjoy a joke together."

Remember the golden rule, the thread that has woven itself through this book. People who excel at using humour to create personal and business success use humour in very specific ways. They use humour to create a connection and to dispel tension. They use humour to build common ground and trust with people they are meeting for the first time, and they use humour to diffuse conflict and help people to relax when they might be nervous or stressed, for example when attending an important meeting or going for a job interview. These excellent Humourologists are not making jokes all day every day. That would make them a clown, a buffoon who doesn't take things seriously. They are not the class clown, squeezing a joke out of every comment to get people to like them. They have learned that humour has power, and as with any source of power, they don't waste it. They use humour in the same way as they use salt, icing sugar or discipline. As little as is necessary, and only when necessary.

Finding the line

One of the most common concerns that people have about using humour in the workplace is their fear of 'crossing the line', of saying something which is ill-judged, tasteless or even offensive. Comedian Marcus Brigstocke has useful advice to share on this point; "Offence is not to be avoided. It's only to be avoided a second or third time. Offence is how I know I care about things. How do I know what I think about something until I hear a counter opinion and recoil from it?" He also tells a story of a joke he used to tell when performing at comedy clubs which had an unintended consequence for one member of the audience. After the show, that person approached Marcus' response was, "Oh, man, I'm so sorry. You write a joke and you think it's funny, and I don't know what to say, can I buy you a drink and he just walked away. I felt monstrous. I felt awful. He came back about half an hour later and he said, you know what, you can buy me that drink. We chatted for a little while and I apologised again and it was okay. You know, I never told the joke again."

You can't find the line without testing it. First, you have to be comfortable with what makes you laugh, what you find funny. Become aware of your own sense of humour. Notice the things which instinctively make you smile. Then, as you practice sharing that humour with others, you'll notice when others respond and when they don't, and you'll notice when you get things wrong, when you cross the line from someone else's point of view. What you experience in this moment is the pang of social rejection, and many people will respond by becoming defensive and even aggressive. I'm sure you've heard people say, "What's the matter with you, can't you take a joke?" Don't be that person. Be like Marcus. Apologise sincerely, learn from it. It's OK to offend someone once. You weren't to know their life story. There's no need to keep doing it, though.

Sir Tony Robinson takes exactly the same approach. "For me, it's about letting go, being open, and taking risks. Not worrying about whether you'll offend somebody, because if you've got your antennae up, you'll know as soon as you start to offend them, you can pull back. If you have offended them too much then you can apologise. So just be who you are, recognise what the interplay is between you and the other person, honour it, play with it, tease it and go further. 99 times out of 100, that does work."

Sitting it out

Professional comedians rarely get it right first time. By the time you hear a joke or a routine on the TV or radio, that script has been practised and refined and honed. Not honed to perfection, because perfection is a static state. Humour is continually evolving. Those routines that you love from your favourite performers started life on the back of a scrap of paper and emerged into the world to be confronted by a barrage of heckling and bottles at a late night comedy club somewhere. One thing that excellent Humourologists have in common with anyone who exhibits excellence in any role is that they are never 'done'. There are always tweaks and improvements to be made, because the world is changing every day. If your competitors are improving, so must you.

One of the things that professional performers will often do with a lacklustre joke is to 'sit it out' and wait for it to become funny. I can think of two examples from films that you may have seen.

The first is in the film *Goodfellas*. Henry Hill, played by Ray Liotta, makes the comment, "You're really funny", to Tommy DeVito, played by Joe Pesci. Tommy is angry at Henry's insinuation, or he pretends to be angry. "Funny like I'm a clown? I amuse you? I make you laugh, I'm here to f**kin' amuse you?" Either way, he pushes Henry for some time and then reveals that it had been a joke. Either it was a practical joke all along, or the humour became a way to diffuse a rapidly escalating situation. The fact that it's hard to tell is integral to Tommy's character and Joe Pesci's superb portrayal of him. The relevance for the Humourologist is that by waiting long enough, the 'joke' became funny.

The second is in the film *Trading Places*. Louis Winthorpe, played by Dan Aykroyd, has been pushed out of his privileged position and replaced by Billy Ray Valentine, played by Eddie Murphy, as part of a bet between two rich brothers. In a restaurant, Billy Ray is giving advice to a business associate as to why he should not take a certain trading position, concluding with, "… and three, judging by the jewels around your girlfriend's neck, I think you're going to need every penny just to keep her happy." The group sit in stunned silence for a few moments. Billy Ray holds his eye contact and keeps a straight face. The subject of the joke then bursts into laughter and everyone around the table follows a moment later. Again, by holding the space and sitting it out, the joke had time to become funny - or the subject chose to interpret it as a joke in order to diffuse the situation and save face.

You'll notice that in both of these examples, the person telling the joke doesn't run away and hide from it if they don't immediately get a standing ovation.

Humourology

Notice also that this is very different from the person who makes an aggressive, insulting or demeaning comment and then, upon seeing his or her 'gang' failing to join in, laughs and claims that they were, "only joking". Using humour in this way just adds to the aggression. Don't do this. The Humourologist never uses humour to attack, only to bring people together. Remember the wise words of Professor Sophie Scott, "Laughter only works if you laugh together".

The overall effect in the *Trading Places* scene is that Billy Ray sets the tone and bonds the group, further alienating Louis who is watching from the street outside. Of course, Billy Ray doesn't know that Louis is watching, he is trying only to connect himself within the immediate group. The Humourologist never uses humour to alienate or isolate, only to connect and bond, and so it's also an important lesson in making sure you know who might be watching or listening. The audience at a comedy club knows what they are letting themselves in for. Your colleagues and clients might not.

How can you judge the appropriateness of your humour?

As before, you start gently and build up.

Too little   **Just right**   **Too much**

This is the natural, innate way that we judge everything in life. Whether you're seasoning your cooking, throwing a ball, painting, adjusting a wobbly table, you gently work your way up to the 'right' result and if you go a little bit over, you know for next time what is 'just right'. In everything we do in life, the only way that we can ever know if we get something right is by testing and gathering feedback. With humour, this starts with something you find funny, and then develops further with what you discover the people around you find funny. Above all else, the Humourologist is an experimenter.

Earlier on in this book, William Hague talked about the use of jokes in political speeches and he mentioned Danny Finkelstein as one of his writing team. Danny tells the same story from a different angle which is always interesting. "William was brilliant at the jokes, he knew the timing of them, he knew the tone, he had the confidence not to use them. One of his rules was, we only use them if they're absolutely, certainly, definitely funny. We wouldn't use one that was maybe only 75% likely to get a laugh, it had to be 100% funny. One of the ways that we used to judge that was - do people laugh when you tell it to them? The test is not, did you think that was funny theoretically? When I tell you that story, do you laugh?"

Ainsley Harriott compares finding the right level with cooking. "I liken it to cooking. Before my onions are caramelised, I've smelt it, I've sensed it so I put a bit of wine in there to save it. It's one of those situations, before something gets completely out of control you realise it's not going well and you save it. We've all done it, we've all been in situations before where we've done gigs, or we're confronted with having to speak in a conference or do something like that. You think this isn't quite going the way I imagined it. Well, experience will tell you how to turn it around a little bit and to have somewhere you can go to bring it back under control."

Somewhere you can go, like a safe place to return to. Perhaps your opening phrase, or the purpose of your presentation, or your intention for the audience. If you keep that in mind, you can always return to it when you have to do what the Holywood types call a 'soft reboot'.

David McCourt shared a story about the late W. Clement Stone, author of the book *Success Through A Positive Mental Attitude*. "During a meeting, he rolled a pencil off the boardroom table as he was talking to me, he bent over and he picked it up. He said, 'You see how an adult can drop a pencil and pick it up without losing their concentration, a little kid would drop a pencil, and then go down on the ground and they might not come back up for five minutes, they find a bug or crumb or they'd find something to do while they're down there. He said, "You have to take everything that's important in your life, and make it so instinctive that you can do it without thinking so that you never have to use any brain power for the things that are instinctive. If you can do it for picking up a pencil then you can do it for the important things and make those things instinctive so they take up none of your brain capacity and none of your energy every day.' It was a really important, important lesson, for me anyway."

And finally... an extreme example of 'sitting it out' from Danny Wallace. "I remember once, it was after a radio recording, they were talking about the old host who had passed away not long before and was a beloved institution. He was in his 80s, a very, very British guy, very reserved, wouldn't show feelings. They were talking about him in such a lovely way. I'd met him a few times and he was great. One lady particularly was saying, 'He found it so hard to talk about love and I was there with him at the end and I just I held his hand and I just kept whispering to him. We all love you. We all love you. That was it. He was gone.'

There was a big long pause. I said, 'It sounds like he might have died of embarrassment.' They all looked at me. I doubled down, I said, 'I'm just saying, it sounds like you killed a man.' Finally, thank God, a laugh came and we could all laugh. It was just about taking that moment of tension and taking a risk with it. Because if it had gone wrong, then they would have just looked at me and said, 'I really think you should leave.' I would have left and I would never have talked to anyone again. But in that moment, it seemed like a risk worth taking."

A risk worth taking. It's important, at times like this, to think about a joke as a risk, and as with any investment, the value of the joke can go down as well as up. However, another thing that humour has in common with investment is that, always, the best thing to do if you're in a risky situation is to wait, because you never know what's in the minds of other people, and you never quite know what could happen next.

A funny thing happened

You might not consider yourself to be a clown or stand-up, and you might think that you're not a natural born joke teller. However, if you have anything in common with 96.8% of people, you'll have a good sense of humour. You will find other things funny - movies, jokes, stories, events in life which bring a smile to your face. Therein lies perhaps your most valuable asset, your most powerful weapon in your defence against the slings and arrows of life. If you have a sense of humour, and if you have survived to this point in life, then you will have experienced amusing events. Maybe at the time they seemed embarrassing or stressful, but looking back, you can easily see the funny side. More than that, you delight in sharing such stories with others. To do so is a powerful social elixir, it brings people together. By sharing our embarrassment, we dilute it. By sharing the lessons that we have learned in life, we help others to avoid them, and by laughing together, we take the sting out of the tale.

Every one of us has made a mistake, done something silly, forgotten something. Instead of hiding our mistakes with arrogance and pretend that they never happened, use them to build your repertoire of funny stories.

Every story that you tell broadcasts information about you. People are remarkably consistent in their stories, so whatever the situation or event, the story is always the same. The edited version that someone chooses to share always shows them in the same way, how they want to be seen by others. They play the hero, villain, problem solver, rule breaker, judge, underdog, genius, inventor or whatever role they admire. Notice the stories that people tell at work on a Monday morning - the same people tell the same stories, every week. Perhaps they had an amazing weekend packed with exciting activities that make their colleagues jealous, or they had a boring weekend because nothing interesting ever happens to them, or they had a weekend in which they had to solve all of their family's problems, or a weekend in which they were ill and nobody thought to check on them.

At this point, you might be wondering, quite rightly, what your stories say about you. You might be thinking about how you edit the stories you tell to put a certain spin on them. Your stories aren't exactly untrue, but they're not the whole truth either.

Instead of telling stories to prove how unlucky, smart or useful you are, consider editing your stories to demonstrate how you're someone who can be relied upon to see the lighter side of life, someone who is fun to have around, someone who can recover from any setback with a smile and a kind word.

Not everyone has a repertoire of ready made funny stories, it's something you have to work at, like building a music collection. You figure out what you like, explore in a certain direction, try something new.

Comedian Milton Jones has evolved his stage persona around 'one liners' rather than stories, however these perform the same role for him, a collection that can be curated and brought out at any opportune moment.

"I ended up doing one liners because I was actually quite nervous, I needed to get as many laughs as possible in as short a time as I could. So if that's what you're aiming at, you end up doing one liners. That's handy for me when I'm doing television, because I get straight to the joke. It's harder when I'm on tour and have to do an hour and 20 minutes show because that is a lot, it's 250 one liners. That's a lot of writing. Even if I go to a party, I might talk for an hour or two but then I need to go to the bottom of the garden and just recollect my thoughts and then come back in again. Making people laugh is a way of pushing the focus back onto them."

Sometimes, a funny story can simply be a close shave, how you thought the worst and were then pleasantly relieved. Empathy makes a shared story into a shared experience, and you'll think, "I'm glad that didn't happen to me!" which is certainly true of Ainsley Harriott's story about a career-defining moment.

"One of my first live TV experiences was on *Good Morning* with Anne Diamond and Nick Owen who were in the kitchen with me. They walked over, I was shaking like a leaf. I'd heated up my pans and everything was ready to go. Anne comes in and asks, 'What are you cooking here?' and grabs hold of the pan. Ouch. Burnt her hand. Well, I thought that was it. I thought my career was over. I couldn't believe it. I burned probably the most recognisable TV presenter at the time in Britain. Everybody loved Anne Diamond. My career was over. It was only the beginning of things. But I tell you what, it just taught me how to prepare and how to get organised. I didn't get sacked, otherwise, I wouldn't be here talking to you. But you know what, I walk into a studio now, I don't even think about it. I plan and get on with it. It's one of the easiest things in the world, yet It's one of the most difficult things in the world, if you haven't done it, so experience is everything."

Would you rather be remembered by your colleagues and friends as someone who found the cloud for every silver lining? Or the person who could always see the funny side of life's calamities? You can choose.

A problem shared...

... is somebody else's problem

Think about stand up comedians who start a routine with "You know how..."

Yes! I know exactly how! Oh my God, that happened to me! I have hairs in my plug hole! My kettle makes a noise like that! I wear shoes!

We all have those experiences. They're just not particularly funny until we all sit in a big room, get drunk and listen to someone else talk about them. We all like to share in the social bonding experience of agreeing that the buses are unreliable and that our kitchen utensils are trying to kill us.

The comedian builds a routine on those experiences by first bringing the audience together in the familiar and then saying what everyone is already thinking. It's the realisation that you're not alone in your crazy thoughts and actions that makes you laugh. Yes, you have a junk drawer in your kitchen with the tops of pens that you no longer own. Yes, you keep the bags of accessories that come with your new roller blind even though you've promised yourself that you will never attempt to do it yourself ever again. Yes, it doesn't matter which way you put the toilet roll on the holder, it's always back to front and takes another three attempts to get it facing forwards. We regard such ordinary experiences as unworthy of a joke until we share them with each other. The scientists who study laughter would describe this as affiliative humour, intended to bring people together by laughing at their common afflictions.

When you see someone suffering, you have a choice. You can point and laugh, like Nelson in *The Simpsons*. Your "Ha-ha!" is at the cost of someone else's pain. You can equally join them, try to help them and make a disarming comment that leaves you both smiling at the fact that the world is out to get you, and at least you're not alone.

State the obvious

My son Sam gazed up at a man who was almost seven feet tall and said, "Wow! It must be fantastic to be so tall".

Often, you might fear insulting someone's intelligence, so you avoid stating the obvious. They surely already know, right? Well, in this case, yes he knew, but he still found it funny. It's the fact that everyone knows but nobody says that makes it funny.

Stating the obvious is actually very important in developing rapport because it lets the other person know that you are sharing the same reality.

I know that it seems obvious to say that you're reading this book, but it's worth saying anyway because I don't want to make any assumptions. For example, someone else might be reading it to you. I find it fascinating that I'm sitting here, at my computer keyboard, and you're there, reading or hearing these words. It's as if I'm writing a personal letter, from me to you, isn't it? When do you think you'll find the time to write back to me?

Stating the obvious draws the audience into your world.

For example, let's say that you are giving a presentation at work and you want to use a cat to illustrate a point, and you want to relate this directly to the audience, so you can say, "Does anyone here have a cat? If not, do you know someone who has a cat? Have you all at least seen a picture of a cat?"

The first question elicits a response, a yes or no. The second gathers more of the audience into the 'yes' group, and the third question can be spoken with a little exasperated humour, which lets the remaining people know that they are safe and normal.

If one person answers, "No!" to the last question, in an attempt to heckle you and grab control, you can say, "then how do you know what a cat is?" or you can even have your joke prepared beforehand by bringing along a picture of a cat to show them.

Agreement builds rapport. In the world of improvised comedy, one of the cardinal rules is to never disagree. Performers must always build on each others' ideas, never kill them. You may have watched children playing 'make believe' games and arguing with each other when they don't follow this rule.

The children's game might go like this:

"I'm a doctor"

"I'm a fighter pilot."

"You can't be a fighter pilot, they don't belong in a hospital."

"This is a flying hospital in a jet fighter."

"No it isn't, it's a hospital in New York and I'm a famous brain surgeon. You can be my patient."

"No, you're my co-pilot."

"No I'm not."

Each child has their own imaginary world and is unwilling to join the other in theirs, or even to merge the two worlds together.

The improvised comedy performance, on the other hand, might go like this:

"I'm a doctor."

"And I'm a fighter pilot."

"And I'm having a fantastic time in your flying hospital. Where are we going?"

"We're flying to New York, Doctor, so that you can perform a life saving operation."

"That's right, a brain surgery operation that will save the life of this banana."

"It's so wonderful that you're a famous brain surgeon, what is the best part of your job."

"It's flying around in flying hospitals like this one. Say, could I try flying it for a while?"

And so on...

The 'build on' rule brings the performers together in the same world, and the bizarre nature of that world creates the humour. The listener's brain has to imagine a flying hospital and a life saving operation on a banana. Trying to cram those unlikely bedfellows into one image creates the tension, or the juxtaposition as they call it in the arts, which leads to laughter. At the very least, a smile. Come on, I'm trying my best here. Maybe you're smiling on the inside.

Stating the obvious, or stating universal truths, is an excellent way to build rapport. It does not insult the other person as long as you're not speaking as if you know something that they don't.

Stating the obvious is akin to sharing a universal truth, something which everyone knows but doesn't talk about, as illustrated by Milton Jones. "When you go and see stand up comedy, what you're seeing is a stylised version of people telling you the truth, hugely exaggerated. One of the first things I ever saw when going to comedy clubs was Eddie Izzard doing a routine about the missiles in the first Iraq war, where they were telling us that these missiles were so technical, so precise and they were only killing bad people. Eddie did this great routine about the missiles being brilliant, they go to the house, they read who's in, they ring the doorbell, they go upstairs, they check and he nailed the whole thing. It was satirical about the government and their lies. That's what we're all thinking, and we can't quite nail it. But you've nailed it and now we're all together."

Stating the obvious is particularly important when you are creating humour out of your own predicament, when you are learning to laugh at yourself as a way of diffusing tension, releasing stress and building social bonds.

Star of the 1990s TV sketch show *The Fast Show* Arabella Weir even based a character on her shortcomings, as all of the members of the cast were encouraged to do, the idea being that there is comedy in truth, and the more uncomfortable the truth, the bigger the laugh. In Arabella's case, we might even say that the bigger the bum, the bigger the laugh.

"My catchphrase was 'Does my bum look big in this?' Take the thing that you are most frightened of the world finding out about you and out it. Yes, I always used to say at the time that I outed my bum. Until that moment, what had happened is I spent my entire life genuinely working out outfits, handbags, ways of getting out of rooms because I was absolutely convinced that not only was it the biggest bum in the world, but that everything pivoted on people not seeing that. Because my entire career, my happiness is predicated on them not knowing that. It was only when we were riffing at the end of the first series and Paul and Charlie said 'Why don't you do someone who's like you?' I said, 'What do you mean like me?' They said, 'Oh, always going on about 'Do I look fat in this? Is my hair wrong?" Imagine somebody being arrested and appearing in court, or whatever it was, if she was still thinking, yeah, never mind about whether I'm guilty or

Humourology

not, look at my hair. Is this too short? Or were these the wrong earrings? So yes, I was outing my greatest fear, rather than trying to pretend I was thin, and had a small bum, which had obviously been a huge effort, because it was a conceit."

What an important piece of advice for any Humourologist - "Take the thing that you are most frightened of the world finding out about you and out it." because if you don't somebody else will, and they might not be so kind. If you're worried that there's something about you that people laugh about behind your back then rest assured - they are. You can either pretend they're not, or you can try to stop them, or you can go with it. You can accept your gift and use it to grow a stronger, more flexible, more powerful funny bone.

⁵The Punchline

"Without humour we're not human."
Robin Ince

And now, the end is here, and so we face the final chapter. But don't be sad, remember what Mike said to Sully at the end of Monsters, Inc. "But, hey… at least we had some laughs, right?"

Right?

I do hope so. In this book I have shared the insights that I've gained, not only from my own work in the performing arts and in business but also those shared with me through the Humourology podcast. My wonderful guests have each brought their own experiences and perspectives and so without them, this book would not have been possible.

What's the big conclusion from all of this? Humour makes life easier? Well, that's obvious, but it's much more than that; humour is what we use to make life easier. Humour is what we do. Humour is how we cope. Humour isn't an accidental by-product of survival, it is our very means of survival, our first line of defence against a world which is becoming increasingly challenging. As a self-defence skill, it can be learned, like any other.

Imagine you're walking down a deserted street, late at night, in a strange and unfamiliar part of town. A hooded figure emerges from an alleyway. You walk faster, he, she or it walks faster. You are cornered. You have the option to do what comes naturally, flailing around in an uncoordinated frenzy, or you can draw upon your black belt in an especially potent martial art. Of course, you would take the training, which is why people join classes to learn from a countless number of martial arts masters. Well, it's the same with your humour. You're born with a sense of humour, just as you're born with the ability to curl up in a ball and whimper. You can either launch a frenzied attack on your dark assailant with a knock-knock joke, or you can turn to your black belt in Humourology and disarm this would-be attacker with a stinging punchline followed by an acerbic yet well observed social commentary. By breaking the ice, you then discover that you had dropped your umbrella and this kind young stranger was rushing to return it to you. You share a moment's shy laughter about your misunderstanding and go your separate ways. What an opportunity for kindness and affiliation! What an opportunity to share a moment of light in the darkness of the night. Maybe you haven't made a lifelong friendship, but for two people, a moment of tension diffused by humour has now become a funny story. Those two people share that story with their friends, who share it with their colleagues and the laughter spreads. Eventually you see that hooded figure on TV, telling a funny story about chasing down a stranger in a dark part of town, armed only with someone else's umbrella.

Humour is not only your birthright, it is your gift, and it's a gift that you can never lose by giving it away, it is a gift which can only ever grow through sharing. Humour is something magical which gets bigger and better the more we use it and the more we share it.

We've seen how politicians use humour to diffuse global conflict, and we've seen how entrepreneurs use humour to build bridges. We've seen how comedians use humour as a social commentary, to connect people and create shared experiences. We've seen how all of this translates into human potential, and how that potential, when realised, is a catalyst for engagement, productivity and profit.

It might seem strange to reduce such a complex and ethereal human gift into the harsh reality of profit, but think of it this way. Profit, for any business, is simply a way of measuring what has been created which didn't exist before. We can measure profit in Pounds or Dollars or Yuan, or we can measure it in kilowatts or ergs or tonnes or litres or laughs.

When you plant a seed in your garden, that seed is a machine which takes chemicals from the soil, the air and the rain and converts those chemicals into another form. It takes carbon dioxide from the air and water from the rain and converts them into sugar with a by-product of oxygen. All you had to do was plant the seed and wait. Nature did the rest. One tiny seed, and after a few weeks or months you got tomatoes or beans or peppers or sunflowers. Your harvest was pure profit, measured not in currency but in the joy of sharing something you've grown yourself with your friends and loved ones.

A joke or a funny story is very much like a seed. You plant it, and in the right conditions it grows all by itself, producing more laughter along the way. Laughter begets laughter. If you want to measure the bottom line of humour in a business then, sure, there's a conversion rate for laugh to Lira, giggle to Guilder, snigger to Shekel.

As you walk through your office, listen out for the music of laughter. It's unmistakeable. If you're not hearing it, something's wrong. Stress doesn't go away but people might be suppressing it, keeping it inside, bottling it up and taking it home. That's very unhealthy. You can't stop the everyday emergencies and catastrophes that people have to deal with in a business. What you can do is approach them with lightness, with mirth, with good humour. You can be a role model for handling life's challenges in a way which inspires others and lets them know that it's safe to see the crazy, the ridiculous, the ludicrous in even the darkest of moments.

When you look back on life, you won't care about how much money you made or how many boats you owned or how impressive your job title sounded. You will care about how much you loved and are loved. You will care about the better world that you have created for your children and for all children. You will care about the laughs you had along the way.

And that, my friend, is all that we can wish for, that at least we had some laughs, right?

Acknowledgements

There are several people who I would like to acknowledge and give a huge 'thank you' to for their part in the creation of this book.

Sam and Henrietta – I love you – thank you for your constant support and inspiration.

Sam – where did those 21 years go? Watching you develop your talent, charm and sense of humour has taught me so much and you still inspire me to learn more.

My mother Helen for her unswerving love and support and for teaching me the values that have held me in good stead throughout my life.

My late father Laszlo whose extraordinary attitude of considering himself lucky - even through wars, uprisings, and refugee camps - whilst constantly maintaining the ability to laugh at life has inspired me and hopefully rubbed off a bit.

This book would not have been possible without all the amazing people who have supported the Humourology podcast - particularly all the fabulous guests.

The podcast, and ultimately this book, were supported by some absolutely fabulous people who are not only friends but believed deeply in the project and invested so much time and love in making it such a success.

My extraordinarily prescient, patient and persistent publisher Peter Freeth and everyone at Genius Media for their professionalism, good humour and support.

My superb podcast producer Simon Banks whose vision and attention to detail are second to none.

The creative director of Humourology Les Hughes whose astonishingly creative mind and stellar ideas have supported and enriched this body of work.

Emma Hughes, the visual director of Humourology who brilliantly manages to see both the bigger picture and the fine detail.

The multimedia maestro David Rose who has been there at every turn to support with a myriad of sensational skills.

All these people embody the best of Humourology by being fun and funny whilst using the power of humour to build relationships, drive performance and just make the world a brighter, better place.

A few other 'thank yous' to colleagues and friends who have inspired, supported and influenced me; especially Professor Tim O'Brien, Brian Colbert, Kate Benson, Dr Richard Bandler, John and Kathleen La Valle and Travis Whitt.

Thanks all for helping me put the fun into business fundamentals.

The Humourology Podcast

This book might not have existed, or certainly it would have been much shorter and less interesting, without the wonderful and generous contributions of the guests of The Humourology Podcast. New podcast episodes are being recorded continually, so this is a snapshot at the time of publication and therefore I am equally grateful to all of my future guests too.

A huge and heartfelt thank you, therefore, to Yasmin Alibhai-Brown, Dr Richard Bandler, Cally Beaton, Mark Bedford, Mark Billingham, Jo Brand, Marcus Brigstocke, Clive Bull, Kevin Cahill, Alastair Campbell, René Carayol, Brian Colbert, Kevin Day, Omid Djalili, Spike Edney, Michael Fenton Stevens, Danny Finkelstein, Matt Forde, David Gower, William Hague, Andy Hamilton, Dr Phil Hammond, Ainsley Harriott, Dominic Holland, Jon Holmes, Georgie Holt, Robin Ince, Guy Jenkin, Dave Johns, Milton Jones, Dillie Keane, Bobby Kerr, Dani Klein Modisett, John La Valle, John Lloyd, James Longman, Penny Mallory, David McCourt, Alistair McGowan, Deborah Meaden, Katrine Moholt, Neil Mullarkey, Jimmy Mulville, Dermot Murnaghan, Jon O'Donnell, John O'Farrell, Tessy Ojo, Giles Paley-Phillips, Marisa Peer, Arlene Phillips, Jon Plowman, Scott Quinnell, Ebony Rainford-Brent, Steve Richards, Tony Robinson, Arthur Smith, Dan Snow, Graham Stuart, Rory Sutherland, John Sweeney, Danny Wallace, Adrian Walsh, Arabella Weir, Rick Wilson and Paul Zenon.

Visit www.paulboross.com to hear the original interviews which contributed to this book and many more by tuning into the Humourology podcast.

Humourology

The Punchline   181

HUMOUR●LOGY PODCAST

Humourology

About Paul

Paul Boross, keynote speaker, aka The Pitch Doctor, specialises in corporate communication. Drawing on a career that has taken him from primetime TV, music and stand-up comedy to production, business, consultancy and motivational psychology, he trains celebrities and executives in the art and craft of communication, leadership and sales.

Paul's frontline experience of performance (his credits include a 10-year stint at London's legendary Comedy Store) and strong commercial instincts enable him to deliver focused and effective training to clients from across the industry spectrum, from the BBC to Barclays via Google, Nestlé, WPP, Virgin and MTV.

Paul regularly lectures all over the world for The Entertainment Masterclasses and media festivals such as MIP, MIPCOM, BCWW, Kristallen and Edinburgh.

Television and radio credits

- Presented the primetime BBC2 series Speed Up Slow Down, which focused on time management and psychology.

- Motivational psychologist for 9 years on Sky's series School of Hard Knocks with Will Greenwood and Scott Quinnell

- Appeared in ITV's Wannabe, advising young people on the psychology of breaking into the TV and the music businesses.

- Appearances in BBC1's The Politics Show.

- Regular contributor to Sky News, BBC Radio Five Live, LBC and BBC Radio London.

Music and comedy credits

- Headline act at London's The Comedy Store, where he performed for over 10 years.

- Founded, with Tony Hawks, the comedy band Morris Minor and The Majors, whose number-one hits included Stutter Rap and This Is The Chorus.

- One half of the comedy singing duo The Calypso Twins with Ainsley Harriott, which had a major hit with World Party.

- Regular guest appearances with The Comedy Store Players on improvisation nights (with Paul Merton and Josie Lawrence, among others).

- Trained with Mike Myers in improvisation skills.

MORRIS MINOR AND THE MAJORS

The Punchline

Humourology

The Punchline

⁶References

Humour is loosely based on truth

Milton Jones

1   Association of Accounting Technicians, 2018

2   Mesmer-Magnus, J., Glew, D.J. and Viswesvaran, C. (2012), "A meta-analysis of positive humor in the workplace", Journal of Managerial Psychology, Vol. 27 No. 2, pp. 155-190. doi.org/10.1108/02683941211199554

3   www.laughlab.co.uk

4   www.ingentaconnect.com/content/sbp/sbp/ 1987/00000015/00000002/art00012

5   Gallup Business Journal, How Employee Engagement Drives Growth, 2012 and Havard Business Review, Developing Employees' Strengths Boosts Sales, Profit, and Engagement, 2016

6   Luthans, F., and Peterson, S. J., The impact of financial and nonfinancial incentives on business unit outcomes over time, Journal of Applied Psychology, 91, 156-165, 2006

7   Tews, Michel and Noe, Does fun promote learning? The relationship between fun in the workplace and informal learning, Journal of Vocational Behavior Volume 98, February 2017, Pages 46-55

8   Eurofound, European Worker Conditions Survey, 2016

9   rework.withgoogle.com/print/guides/5721312655835136/

10   Facial attractiveness: evolutionary based research Phil Trans R Soc B June 12, 2011 366: 1638-1659.

11   www.jstor.org/stable/3033903

12   Cialdini, R. Influence: The Psychology of Persuasion. HarperCollins, 2009

13   Julie C. Driebe, Morgan J. Sidari, Michael Dufner, Juliane M. von der Heiden, Paul C. Bürkner, Lars Penke, Brendan P. Zietsch, Ruben C. Arslan (2021). Intelligence can be detected but is not found attractive in videos and live interactions. www.psychologytoday.com/us/blog/the-asymmetric-brain/202106 /is-humor-or-intelligence-more-attractive-potential-mate?amp

14   Valeriani, R. Travels with Henry, 1979. Houghton Mifflin, Boston

15   Viveka Adelsward and Britt-Marie Oberg, "The Function of Laughter and Joking in Negotiation Activities," Humor - International Journal of Humor Research 11, 4 (2009), 411.

16   Karen O'Quin and Joel Aronoff, "Humor as a Technique of Social
      Influence," Social Psychology Quarterly 44, 4 (1981), 349.

17   Roger Fisher and William Ury, Getting to Yes: Negotiating
      Agreement without Giving In (New York: Penguin, 2011). 30.

18   www.thebritishacademy.ac.uk/podcasts/10-minute-talks-why-
      laughter-matters

19   neurosciencenews.com/humor-news-sharing-17545

20   royalsocietypublishing.org/doi/abs/10.1098/rspb.2011.1373

21   "A systematic review of humour-based strategies for addressing
      public health priorities" by Elaine Miller, Heidi J. Bergmeier, Claire
      Blewitt, Amanda O'Connor, Helen Skouteris. Australian and New
      Zealand Journal of Public Health

22   Rutter, M. (1985). Resilience in the face of adversity: Protective
      factors and resistance to psychiatric disorder. The British Journal of
      Psychiatry, 147, 598–611

23   Tugade, M. M., & Fredrickson, B. L. (2004). Resilient Individuals
      Use Positive Emotions To Bounce Back From Negative Emotional
      Experiences. Journal Of Personality And Social Psychology, 86(2),
      320–333.

24   Wolin, S. J., & Wolin, S. (1993). The Resilient Self: How Survivors
      of Troubled Families Arise above Adversity. New York: Villard
      Books.

25   Valeriani, R. Travels with Henry, 1979. Houghton Mifflin, Boston

Abel E. and Kruger M. (2010) Smile Intensity in Photographs Predicts
Longevity, Psychological Science, 21, 542–544.

Blanchard, A., Stewart, O. J., Cann, A., & Follman, L. (2014). Making
sense of humor at work. The Psychologist Manager Journal, 17(1), 49-70.
https://doi.org/10.1037/mgr0000011

Cann, A., & Calhoun, L. G. (2001). Perceived personality associations
with differences in sense of humor: Stereotypes of hypothetical others
with high or low senses of humor. HUMOR: International Journal of
Humor Research, 14, 117-130. https://doi.org/10.1515/humr.14.2.117

Cann, A., Calhoun, L. G., & Banks, J. S. (1997). On the role of humor
appreciation in interpersonal attraction. HUMOR: International Journal

of Humor Research, 10, 77-89.
https://doi.org/10.1515/humr.1997.10.1.77

Cann, A., Calhoun, L. G., & Nance, J. (2000). Exposure to humor before or after an unpleasant stimulus: Humor as a preventative or a cure. HUMOR: International Journal of Humor Research, 13, 177-191. https://doi.org/10.1515/humr.2000.13.2.177

Cann, A. T., & Cann, A. (February, 2014). Funny you should say that: Do humor styles map onto humor appreciation? Poster presented at the Society for Personality and Social Psychology Convention, Austin, TX.

Cann, A., & Etzel, K. C. (2008). Remembering and anticipating stressors: Positive personality mediates the relationship with sense of humor. HUMOR: International Journal of Humor Research, 21, 157-178. https://doi.org/10.1515/HUMOR.2008.008

Cann, A., Holt, K., & Calhoun, L. G. (1999). The roles of humor and sense of humor in responses to stressors. HUMOR: International Journal of Humor Research, 12, 177-193. https://doi.org/10.1515/humr.1999.12.2.177

Cann, A., & Matson, C. (2014). Sense of humor and social desirability: Understanding how humor styles are perceived. Personality and Individual Differences, 66, 176-180. https://doi.org/10.1016/j.paid.2014.03.029

Cann, A., Stilwell, K., & Taku, K. (2010). Humor styles, positive personality, and health. Europe's Journal of Psychology, 6(3), 213-235. https://doi.org/10.5964/ejop.v6i3.214

Cann, A., Watson, A. J., & Bridgewater, E. A. (2014). Assessing humor at work: The Humor Climate Questionnaire. HUMOR: International Journal of Humor Research, 27(2), 307-323. https://doi.org/10.1515/humor-2014-0019

Cann, A., Zapata, C. L., & Davis, H. B. (2009). Positive and negative styles of humor in communication: Evidence for the importance of considering both styles. Communication Quarterly, 57(4), 452-468. https://doi.org/10.1080/01463370903313398

Cann, A., Zapata, C. L., & Davis, H. B. (2011). Humor style and relationship satisfaction in dating couples: Perceived versus self-reported humor styles as predictors of satisfaction. HUMOR: International Journal of Humor Research, 24(1), 1-20. https://doi.org/10.1515/humr.2011.001

Crawford, S. A., & Caltabiano, N. J. (2011). Promoting emotional well-being through the use of humor. The Journal of Positive Psychology, 6,

237-252. https://doi.org/10.1080/17439760.2011.577087

Greengross, G., Martin, R. A., & Miller, G. (2012). Personality traits, intelligence, humor styles, and humor production ability of professional stand-up comedians compared to college students. Psychology of Aesthetics, Creativity, and the Arts, 6(1), 74-82. https://doi.org/10.1037/a0025774

Hatfield, Elaine; Cacioppo, John T.; Rapson, Richard L. Clark, Margaret S. (Ed), (1992). Primitive emotional contagion. Emotion and social behavior. Review of personality and social psychology, Vol. 14., (pp. 151-177). Thousand Oaks, CA, US: Sage Publications, Inc, xi, 311 pp.

Leist, A. K., & Müller, D. (2013). Humor types show different patterns of self-regulation, self-esteem and well-being. Journal of Happiness Studies, 14(2), 551-569. https://doi.org/10.1007/s10902-012-9342-6

Martin, R. A., Puhlik-Doris, P., Larsen, G., Gray, J., & Weir, K. (2003). Individual differences in uses of humor and their relation to psychological well-being: Development of the Humor Styles Questionnaire. Journal of Research in Personality, 37(1), 48-75. https://doi.org/10.1016/S0092-6566(02)00534-2

McGhee, P. E. (1999). Health, healing and the amuse system: Humor as survival training (3rd ed.). Dubuque, IA: Kendall/Hunt Publishing.

Mesmer-Magnus, J., Glew, D. J., & Viswesvaran, C. (2012). A meta-analysis of positive humor in the workplace. Journal of Managerial Psychology, 27(2), 155-190. https://doi.org/10.1108/02683941211199554

Mussman, S., Clontz, C., Cann, A., & Calhoun, L. G. (1993). Humor and depression: Is laughter good medicine? Paper presented at the meeting of the Southeastern Psychological Association, Atlanta, GA.

Ruch, W. (2013). Benevolent and corrective humor. Presentation at the 13th International Summer School and Symposium on Humor and Laughter, Magdeburg, Germany.

Seaward BL. Managing Stress: Principles and Strategies for Health and Well-Being. Sudbury, Mass.: Jones and Bartlett; 2009:258.

Ingram Content Group UK Ltd.
Milton Keynes UK
UKHW011124150623
423488UK00006B/182

9 781908 293633